30 day adventure to

Know Jesus
more!

30 day adventure to
Know Jesus *more!*

NRJOHNSON

30 DAY ADVENTURE TO KNOW JESUS MORE

© 2024 by NRJohnson

Published by Deeper Christian Press | Windsor, Colorado

Paperback ISBN: 978-1-953549-08-2
EBook ISBN: 978-1-953549-09-9

Cover photo © by Prixel Creative / Lightstock

All rights reserved. No part of this publication may be reproduced in any form unless it is used for the furtherance of the Gospel and/or for the glory of Christ Jesus (i.e., not for personal gain). We ask that you do not reproduce the publication as a whole, but you are permitted to reproduce and distribute this material in unaltered excerpts, as long as you offer it freely—free of any charges (except necessary distribution costs) and with this statement included. Any exceptions to the above must be approved by deeperChristian.

· · · · ·

Unless otherwise indicated, Scripture quotations are taken from the (LSB®) Legacy Standard Bible®, Copyright © 2021 by The Lockman Foundation. Used by permission. All rights reserved. Managed in partnership with Three Sixteen Publishing Inc. LSBible.org and 316publishing.com.

Scripture quotations marked NASB are from the (NASB®) New American Standard Bible®, Copyright © 1960, 1971, 1977, 1995 by The Lockman Foundation. Used by permission. All rights reserved. lockman.org. | Scripture quotations marked ESV are from the ESV Bible® (The Holy Bible, English Standard Version®), copyright © 2001 by Crossway Bibles, a publishing ministry of Good News Publishers. Used by permission. All rights reserved. | Scripture quotations marked NKJV are from New King James Version®. Copyright © 1982 by Thomas Nelson. Used by permission. All rights reserved. | Scripture quotations marked AMP are taken from the Amplified® Bible (AMP), Copyright © 2015 by The Lockman Foundation. Used by permission. lockman.org. | Scripture quotations marked ISV are taken from the Holy Bible: International Standard Version® Release 2.0. Copyright © 1996-2013 by the ISV Foundation. Used by permission of Davidson Press, LLC. All rights reserved internationally. | Scripture quotations marked CSB are taken from the Christian Standard Bible®, Copyright © 2017 by Holman Bible Publishers. Used by permission.

Bold and/or italicized text in Scripture quotations indicates author's emphasis.

· · · · ·

deeperChristian.com
This ministry is maintained by the Lord through the stewardship of those who value it.

CONTENTS

DAY

1	I Want to Know Him More	7
2	Knowing Jesus Through His Word	13
3	The 7Rs of Relationship	21
4	Knowing Jesus Through His Names	27
5	Yahweh	33
6	Elohim	43
7	Sweetness to the Soul	51
8	Experience Heartburn	55
9	Jehovah Jireh	59
10	Renewing Our Minds	65
11	Jehovah Rapha	73
12	Be Like a Cow	81
13	Jehovah Shalom	87
14	I Raise My Ebenezer	93
15	El Olam	97
16	Lord, Teach Us to Pray	105
17	Jehovah Raah + Adonai	111
18	Extravagant Forgiveness	123
19	Extravagant Forgiveness Too	127
20	Jehovah Mekoddishkem	133
21	All In on Jesus	141

22	Loving Our Neighbors	145
23	Study for Yourself	155
24	Undistracted Devotion	159
25	Obsession	165
26	Qannā	169
27	What Describes You?	177
28	Jehovah Shammah	181
29	As Ointment Poured Forth	185
30	What's Next?	199
	Endnotes	203

DAY 01

I WANT TO KNOW HIM MORE

Back in the early 1980s, Steve Fry penned this chorus, which was made famous by musician Steve Green:

> Oh, I want to know You more!
> Deep within my soul I want to know You,
> Oh, I want to know You.
> To feel Your heart and know Your mind,
> Looking in Your eyes stirs up within me,
> Cries that says I want to know You
> Oh, I want to know You more.
> Oh, I want to know You more.

The song concludes with this phrase:

> And I would give my final breath
> To know You in Your death and resurrection
> Oh I want to know You more

This declaration should be the cry of our hearts toward Jesus: "Oh, I want to know you more!"

Welcome, officially, to the *30 Day Adventure to Know Jesus More*.

Over these next 30 days, we will intentionally draw near to God and discover the delight of knowing Him (see James 4:8 and Philippians 3:10).

THE PROMISE

Hebrews 11:6 provides a fantastic promise for us to embrace during this 30-day adventure (and for the rest of our lives): "But without faith it is impossible to please Him, for he who comes to God must believe that He is, and that He is a rewarder of those who *diligently* seek Him" (NKJV).

Did you catch the promise?

God is a rewarder…of those who diligently seek Him.

And more amazingly, the reward we get is not riches or fame but the very thing we seek. Our reward is God Himself. We seek Him, and He gives us Himself.

So that is what we will do—diligently seek after God and find Him a rewarder. Our goal is not to get something *from* God but to know Him more.

KNOWING HIM

One of my favorite words in Greek is γινώσκω (ginōskō). This word appears all over the New Testament, and it typically emphasizes knowing something through experience, relationship, or intimacy. If you want to know something academically, there's a different word for that. But this word is different; it bespeaks of an experiential and depth of knowledge.

In describing what eternal life is, Jesus said in

John 17:3, "And this is eternal life, that they may *know* [ginōskō] You, the only true God, and Jesus Christ whom You have sent."

Having eternal life is not about knowing information about Jesus or passing a true/false test, but about actually knowing (ginōskō) God—it is having a relationship with Him and experiencing His life.

While academic knowledge isn't bad, it won't save you.

James reminds us, "You believe that God is one. You do well; the demons also believe, and shudder" (James 2:19). Head knowledge is important, but it won't get you into heaven.

What saves us? It is only through believing and putting our faith in our Lord Jesus Christ. But more than a mental belief, salvation comes down to relationship.

In a rather scary passage of Scripture, Jesus talks with a group of people who went to church and did a bunch of impressive religious activities... but in the end, His statement to them was, "I never *knew* you; depart from Me, you who practice lawlessness" (Matthew 7:23). The word "knew" in the passage is *ginōskō*. Here was a group of religious people whose lives were full of religious activities, but despite their actions, they did not have a relationship with Jesus, so they were cast out.

THE ADVENTURE

The next 30 days are not about attempting to fit in another religious activity or duty. Our desire throughout the entire "adventure" is to keep our focus steadfast upon Jesus and deepen our intimacy with Him. While there will be things to do and study, the emphasis is to know (ginōskō) Jesus more by spending time with Him (not filling your schedule with more activities). This is about being WITH God, not doing things FOR Him.

One of the greatest challenges I've faced in life and ministry is guarding my intimacy *with* Jesus and not excusing it to do ministry *for* Jesus. And I've found there is a vast difference between the two.

I encourage you to declare anew in your soul, "Jesus, I want to know you more. Deep within my soul I want to know You. Oh, I want to know You more!"

THE NEXT 30 DAYS

As you journey throughout this thirty-day adventure, you will have something to read and often something practical to do. But again, this is less about things to "do" and more about giving you ideas of how to "be" with Jesus.

Are you ready?

These next 30 days have the potential to radically change your life and deepen your intimacy with Jesus—not because of anything I write, but because you are intentionally taking time these next 30 days to pursue Him. And remember, He is a rewarder of those who do that.

GO DEEPER

Each day has a "Go Deeper" section, which gives you something practical to do today to know Jesus more . . . and will provide additional resources or materials if you want to study that day's concept further.

1. Read the following passages and then spend time with Jesus. Don't feel like you have to "do" something as much as just spend time with Him. Express your heart and tell Him your desire to know Him more. Commit yourself to diligently seeking Him for the next 30 days (and my hope is for the rest of your life).

    - **Deuteronomy 6:4–5** – "Hear, O Israel! Yahweh is our God, Yahweh is one! You shall love Yahweh your God with all your heart and with all your soul and with all your might."
    - **Matthew 22:36–40** – "Teacher, which is the great commandment in the Law?" And He said to him, "'YOU SHALL LOVE THE LORD YOUR GOD WITH ALL YOUR HEART, AND WITH ALL YOUR SOUL, AND WITH ALL YOUR MIND.' This is the great and foremost commandment. And the second is like it, 'YOU SHALL LOVE YOUR NEIGHBOR AS YOURSELF.' On these two commandments hang the whole Law and the Prophets."
    - **Psalm 84:1–2, 10** – How lovely are Your dwelling places, O Yahweh of hosts! My soul has longed and even fainted for the courts of Yahweh; my heart and my flesh sing for joy to the living God.... For better is a day in Your courts than a thousand elsewhere. I would choose to stand at the threshold of the house of my God than dwell in the tents of wickedness.
    - **Jeremiah 29:13–14** – "You will seek Me and find Me when you search for Me with all your heart. 'I will be found by you,' declares Yahweh, 'and I will

return your fortunes and will gather you from all the nations and from all the places where I have banished you,' declares Yahweh, 'and I will cause you to return to the place from where I sent you into exile.'"
- **Hebrews 11:6** – And without faith it is impossible to please Him, for he who draws near to God must believe that He is and that He is a rewarder of those who seek Him.
- **Matthew 6:33** – "But seek first His kingdom and His righteousness, and all these things will be added to you."

2. If you'd like to study this concept of "ginōskō" further, check out episode 87 (called *Do You KNOW Jesus or Merely Know ABOUT Jesus?*) on my Deeper Christian Podcast or read the book *Knowing Jesus*. You can find all the links and bonus resources for this book by going to deeperChristian.com/30day.

3. Corrie ten Boom once said, "Beware the barrenness of a busy life." While she isn't referring to passivity or inactivity, how does this warning give insight into your pursuit of knowing Christ?

DAY 02

KNOWING JESUS THROUGH HIS WORD

Yesterday, we began discussing knowing Jesus and diligently seeking Him (remember, He is a rewarder of those who do so; see Hebrews 11:6).

While there are many ways we can seek after and know Jesus more, the foundation to knowing Christ is through His Word.

As such, Scripture is essential to our growth and maturity as Christians. It is critical for our understanding of and intimacy with Jesus. Genuine Christian discipleship hinges upon God's Word. But, again, the primary reason we get into Scripture is that we want to grow in intimacy, oneness, and relationship with the Author.

THE WRITTEN AND LIVING WORD

There is a powerful interaction between the Written Word of God (the Bible) and the Living Word of God (Jesus).

John reminds us at the beginning of his gospel that...

DAY 02

In the beginning was the Word, and the Word was with God, and the Word was God. He was in the beginning with God. All things came into being through Him, and apart from Him nothing came into being that has come into being. In Him was life, and the life was the Light of men.... And the Word became flesh, and dwelt among us, and we beheld His glory, glory as of the only begotten from the Father, full of grace and truth (John 1:1–4, 14).

Jesus is the Living Word. He is the Word made flesh. He is the fullness, the culmination, and the lived-out expression of the Written Word. And everything throughout the Old and New Testaments is fulfilled in Him (see Matthew 5:17–18).

And, again, there is an interaction between the Written and Living Word—though distinct and separate, the Written Word leads us, by the Holy Spirit, into the Living Word. And as you get to know the Written Word, you get to know the Living Word even better.

Reading, memorizing, and studying the Bible isn't about some academic endeavor; rather, it is about getting to know the Author. Academics are not bad (and we *should* know the Bible academically), but the primary purpose of Bible study is to know Jesus and be transformed by truth.[1]

Therefore, we must make the shift in approaching Scripture from mere academics to intimately knowing God Himself and allowing Him to change our lives.

When we see the Word as living, active, and sharper than a double-edged sword that wants to do its work in our lives (see Hebrews 4:12), we will continue to hunger and delight in it, even when it is difficult and painfully pierces (changes) our lives.

Simply, if we want a greater level of intimacy with Jesus, we must be in the Word! If we desire to know Him better, we need to soak and saturate within the pages of Scripture.

Again, our goal is to know God intimately and deeply (see John 17:3) and have the desire to "know Him and the power of His resurrection and the fellowship of His sufferings, being conformed to His death" (Philippians 3:10).

So, how do Christians interact with the Bible for spiritual growth? How do we build our lives around Jesus Christ by getting into His Word?

THE SEVEN RS OF RELATIONSHIP

While not exhaustive, there are seven key ways to interact with God's Word, which leads to deeper growth and intimacy; I call them the seven Rs of relationship. If you do them to *know* (ginōskō) Jesus Christ, they will lead you into a richer relationship and closeness with Him.

Today, we will look at the first three and examine the final four tomorrow.

1. READ
Read God's Word

Reading God's Word is essential to the Christian life. If we truly believe the Bible is God's words (which it is), we should delight in spending time in it.

Yet most of us treat Scripture like our English literature textbook in high school—it's there when we have to look at it; otherwise, it makes a great doorstop. But God's Word is not Shakespeare or Whitman; it is the very words of our King. His Word says that it is living and active (see Hebrews 4:12) and that we should delight ourselves in it (see Psalm 119:16, 24) because it is sweeter than honey (see Psalm 19:10 and 119:103).

Charles Spurgeon, the great prince of preachers, once declared:

> *True Bible-readers and Bible-searchers never find it wearisome. They like it least who know it least, and they love it most who read it most. They find it newest who have known it longest, and they find the pasture to be the richest whose souls have been the longest fed upon it.*[2]

Do you read God's Word? If not, I would encourage you to get into a daily habit of basking in the richness of His truth. Even if you are a slow reader, you can read through the entire Bible in a year if you commit to about ten minutes daily.[3]

2. RETAIN
Memorize God's Word

Many of us cringe when we hear the word "memorize." Memorization has been difficult for me throughout the years, but I've found that when I write God's Word upon my heart, it transforms my thinking and daily living.

We live in a time when memory isn't needed much.

We have Google and our smartphones to do the hard thinking for us. And yet, while we may not use our brains as often as we should, they have incredible power to think, reason, and memorize. God made our brains capable of storing information and quickly retrieving it when necessary. You are not at a disadvantage in the memory department.

I once challenged a group of teens to memorize a lengthy Bible passage. Most balked and complained, declaring they couldn't remember a passage that long. Yet, these same individuals who reportedly could not memorize Scripture were the same teens who could quote large sections from the latest movie, could sing the lyrics to countless songs, and had sports statistics memorized for numerous athletes.

We *can* memorize, but the reality is that we only remember things we deem important and valuable— or that which is repetitive and gets stuck in our minds whether we want it to or not.[4]

3. RUMINATE
Study God's Word

Reading God's Word is not a substitute for *studying* God's Word. While reading the Bible is essential, you should also have a plan to study Scripture. As it has been said, we should read the Bible for breadth and study it for depth. Going beyond the surface and into the depths of Bible study will open up the text and your understanding in ways you never thought possible. And studying God's Word doesn't have to be complicated—it is easier than you think (though it will take work).

One of the most rewarding and transformational things I have done in the past decade is to study Scripture. It has increased my understanding of and love for truth, given me a vision for living a godly life, and given me an incredible passion for Jesus Christ.

Remember, the reason we get into the Word is not for mere academics but to know Jesus. Even in Bible study, the purpose isn't just head knowledge but greater intimacy and relationship with God Himself.

GO DEEPER

1. Consider how you can practically apply these first three R's in your life. How can you tweak your daily schedule to make time for God's Word?

2. Spend time with the Living Word (Jesus) and ask Him to give you greater insight into His Written Word (Bible)—not for information but for transformation and intimacy.

3. Read John 16:7–15 below. Why is it a benefit that Jesus went to the Father and sent us the Holy Spirit? According to Jesus, what are several things the Holy Spirit will do? How does this relate to knowing the Word and Jesus more?

> *"But I tell you the truth, it is to your advantage that I go away; for if I do not go away, the Advocate will not come to you; but if I go, I will send Him to you.*

And He, when He comes, will convict the world concerning sin and righteousness and judgment; concerning sin, because they do not believe in Me; and concerning righteousness, because I go to the Father and you no longer see Me; and concerning judgment, because the ruler of this world has been judged. I still have many more things to say to you, but you cannot bear them now. But when He, the Spirit of truth, comes, He will guide you into all the truth; for He will not speak from Himself, but whatever He hears, He will speak; and He will disclose to you what is to come. He will glorify Me, for He will take of Mine and will disclose it to you. All things that the Father has are Mine; therefore I said that He takes of Mine and will disclose it to you."

4. If you want to get started, I encourage you to read Colossians. Remember to read it with the desire to know the Author, not just gain information. Colossians is an incredible book focused on the preeminence of Jesus Christ.

DAY 03

THE 7Rs OF RELATIONSHIP

Yesterday, we looked at the first three R's to know Jesus more through His Word.
For a quick review, we looked at:
1. **Read** (Read God's Word)
2. **Retain** (Memorize God's Word)
3. **Ruminate** (Study God's Word)

Let's dive into the last four...

4. RELISH
Delight In God's Word

God is clear that we are to delight in His Word. Reading and studying the Bible is not a punishment; it should be one of our greatest joys and one of the things we look forward to most. Never once have I looked at a piece of dark chocolate and cringed, wishing I didn't have to eat it—I always delight in partaking in its chocolatey goodness.

The Psalmist explained this concept using the sweetest thing he knew about...honey. But if I may take the liberty to turn it into 21st-century chocolate language, the Psalmist says:

> *How sweet are Your words to my taste,*
> *Sweeter than chocolate in my mouth!*
> *Psalm 119:103 (paraphrased)*

God's Word tells us we are to relish it. It is to be our delight and joy because it reveals truth (Jesus Christ) and thus gives us life.

As Jesus declared in John 14:6, "I am the way, and the truth, and the life. No one comes to the Father but through Me."

Do you treasure God's Word? Do you come to Scripture with joy?

5. RECITE
Declare God's Word

God's Word has an extraordinary aspect: when you read, study, and are transformed by its truth, you can't hold it in! Scripture creates a volcano of truth within your life that needs to come out.

You may not be called to be a preacher or a teacher—two obvious ways of declaring God's Word—but everyone who spends time in God's Word will desire to declare it. This isn't "declare it or else;" instead, this is similar to viewing an incredible sunset.

When we behold a breathtaking sunset, a "wow" escapes our lips. We don't try; it just comes out. The same is true when we get into Scripture—when we see Jesus as He is and when His Word transforms our lives, we can't help but tell others.

Whether you have the opportunity to preach, teach, write, evangelize, or tell your friends and family about the truth God is using to transform your life, declaring God's Word is vital to your spiritual growth for two key reasons.
1. Declaring God's Word clarifies and gives us language for what God is doing in us. As we communicate truth, our thinking becomes more clear, and we understand the truth better. It has long been said that one of the best ways to learn something is to teach it.
2. Declaring God's Word is an opportunity for God to use you to share His truth and turn the world upside down. Our lives as Christians are not like a bottle kept on a shelf, a candle hidden beneath a basket, or salt left in a salt shaker. If Scripture and the Gospel are authentic in our lives, it will come out of us—not because we are forced to preach or evangelize, but because we can't help ourselves.

As you come to Scripture, will you allow God to use your life and lips to declare the wonders and truth of the glorious Gospel?

6. REST
Build Your Life Upon God's Word

A house "rests" on its foundation. If the foundation is weak, the building will be weak.

Scripture is our foundation, our bedrock, for living. It is the truth we boldly stand upon. It is the standard the Holy Spirit uses to test us. It is God's very words, which all point to Jesus Christ and His work upon the Cross.

Many of us know Hebrews 4:12, which says, "For the word of God is living and active and sharper than any two-edged sword, and piercing as far as the division of soul and spirit, of both joints and marrow, and able to judge the thoughts and intentions of the heart." Yet interestingly, the verse sits in a section all about "rest."

Hebrews 4 opens with the promise of entering God's rest. Using the Old Testament picture of the Israelites entering the Promised Land and finding rest, the writer of Hebrews talks about the promise for believers to live in a state of rest. Then, he transitions and talks about God's Word.

I find it fascinating that there is a connection between God's Word and the rest I experience in Jesus Christ. Like a hospital operating table that I rest upon to allow the surgeon to take his scalpel and make cuts in my body so that healing and transformation can take place, so too I rest upon God's Word and allow the Holy Spirit to take His Word (a double-edged sword or scalpel) and pierce my life so that I might be transformed and shaped into His likeness.

I must have a foundation upon which to rest and build my life. I need unchanging truth to be the guide of my life. I need security, a rock beneath my feet, to endure the trials and temptations I face daily. As a Christian, my foundation is Jesus Christ and His unchanging Word. He does not change and cannot lie, nor can His Word—it is a sure promise I can take to the bank.

7. RESPOND
Be Transformed by God's Word

Ultimately, my goal is to be transformed into Christ's likeness. I, who once walked in darkness, am to walk in the light, and I need the powerful, enabling work of the Holy Spirit to take my heart of darkness and change my very nature and character. It is not enough to have the outward appearance of being different; I must become transformed on the inside, which I cannot do in and of myself.

The key to Christlikeness is to respond to the Word and allow the Spirit of God to transform me. I cannot approach God's Word with arms folded in an "I-have-it-all-together" and "I-don't-need-anything" attitude. I must come humbly, surrendered, arms open, willing to respond to the truth, and desire the Holy Spirit to do His work within me.

When I have an attitude of response—the desire to be transformed and a willingness to obey—then I won't remain the same when I get into Scripture. Since Scripture is a double-edged sword, I will be cut and changed as I get close to it.

Will you approach Scripture with the desire to "attain to the unity of the faith, and of the full knowledge of the Son of God, to a mature man, to the measure of the stature which belongs to the fullness of Christ" (Ephesians 4:13)? Will you allow the Word of God to be the measuring rod in your life that the Holy Spirit tests you against? Will you rest upon and respond to Scripture so He can transform your heart and mind (see Romans 8:29; 12:1–2; 2 Corinthians 3:17–18, 5:17; Colossians 1:13–14; 1 John 2:5–6, 3:2–3)?

GO DEEPER

1. Carve out some time today to delight in Jesus and spend time with Him—talking, listening, and discovering that "[He makes] known to me the path of life; in [His] presence is fullness of joy; at [His] right hand there are pleasures forever" (see Psalm 16:11).

2. If you didn't read through Colossians yesterday, I encourage you to do that. If you have, consider reading it through again, perhaps in a different Bible translation.

DAY 04

KNOWING JESUS THROUGH HIS NAMES

The previous two days, we looked at knowing Jesus through His Word.

As Christians, the Word must become foundational in our pursuit of Christ.

Today, I want to examine another way we can know Jesus more…

WHAT'S IN A NAME? A LOT.

While Shakespeare proclaimed that a rose by any other name would be as sweet, the truth is that a lot is contained in a name.

Names throughout the Bible were more than just names; they conveyed something about the person—typically showcasing their heart, nature, character, reputation, and/or lifestyle.

For example, Jacob was born holding onto the heel of his twin brother Esau; therefore, they gave him the name "Jacob." Interestingly, the name also portrayed Jacob's life: he was a liar, deceiver, and manipulator (all aspects of what it meant to be a "heel-grabber" in that culture).

This is why it is so significant when God changes someone's name, for it isn't just their name He is changing, but their identity, character, nature, and heart.

In Genesis 32, Jacob wrestled with God throughout the night, and by daybreak, he received a limp and a new name. He renamed the location Peniel (again, another name change) because he saw the face of God, and Jacob's name was forever Israel.

What started as a man known for lying, deceiving, and manipulating became a man radically changed because he came face-to-face with God. His life was transformed to the point that God changed his name to Israel (meaning "the one who wrestles/contends with God" or "the prince of God"). Jacob's identity, character, and life were altered.

GOD'S NAMES

It's not by accident, then, that throughout the Bible, one way God reveals His nature, attributes, character, life, and identity is by telling us His names.

Again, the names of God aren't merely a "name" but a revelation of who He is.

One incredible way to know Jesus more is to understand His names.

Let me add an additional thought. God's nature doesn't change (see the "Go Deeper" section for Scripture passages). So when God reveals His names, they are not something He once *was*; instead, they portray who *He was, is, and forever will be.*

For example, one of God's names is *Jehovah Jireh*, the Lord Who Provides. This means that God not only provided the ram in Isaac's place for Abraham's sacrifice (see Genesis 22:13–14) but also that God is still and will forever be a provider. This is His nature.

So, as you learn and understand God's names, we must remember that this is who He still is! What an incredible reality!

Let's discuss two aspects related to God's name…

1. HALLOWED

While teaching His disciples to pray, Jesus begins by making an interesting declaration. He says: "Pray, then, in this way: 'Our Father who is in heaven, hallowed be Your name…'" (Matthew 6:9).

What is known as the "Lord's Prayer" begins with taking the Father's name and *hallowing* it.

The word "hallow" means to honor as holy, to be kept as holy, or to be treated with reverence.

Why are we called to hallow God's name and keep it holy? Because it's more than a name—it's His identity, life, character, reputation, and nature. To degrade His name is to dishonor and debase His person (which is why one of the Ten Commandments is not to take the Lord's name in vain).

So, as we pray, Jesus tells us that we are to give honor and reverence to WHO God is (not merely thank Him for the things He provides). And as we meditate upon and revere God, we soon discover that we can't help but worship Him. As such, we are to guard the holiness of His great name (i.e., His character, life, reputation, etc.).

2. OUR PLACE OF REFUGE

Proverbs, the book of wisdom, tells us, "The name of Yahweh is a strong tower; the righteous runs into it and is set securely on high" (18:10).

Where do we find our safety, security, and refuge through the storms and struggles of life? We find it in the name of Yahweh—because it's more than a name; it's His very presence and person.

Where do you turn when things get tough in your life or when fear knocks on your door? What do you hold tight to as your hope? If it is anything but God Himself, then that place or thing has become an idol in your life. It may not be a Buddha statue, but biblically, you have turned and placed your hope in something false, what God declares as idolatry. And we are told throughout Scripture to flee idolatry and turn only to the Lord our God (see as examples: Exodus 20:3–6; Leviticus 19:4; Judges 10:13–14; Psalm 135:15–18; Isaiah 44:9–20; 45:20; 1 Corinthians 10:14; Galatians 5:19–21; Colossians 3:5; 1 John 5:21).

What if Jesus was your first turn?

What if trouble caused you to run toward Jesus and find your refuge, safety, and salvation in His name? Amazingly, the name "Jesus" literally means "Yahweh is salvation" in Hebrew. For that is who Jesus is—our salvation.

If you've found yourself turning to any other "name" other than Jesus, I encourage you to repent, turn toward Christ, and allow Him to be all you need for life and godliness (see 2 Peter 1:3–4), for it is only in Him where we find our refuge and strength, our hope in times of trouble.

BEHOLD HIM

Throughout this 30-day adventure, we will examine some of the names of God in Scripture. While there are dozens to explore, we will focus on a few key names He gives throughout the Old Testament, which find their fulfillment in Jesus—with the desire to know Him more.

GO DEEPER

1. Consider the following passages about the fact that God's nature does not change. How do these passages encourage you to trust in our God? How do they help you get to know Jesus more?

- **Numbers 23:19** – God is not a man, that He should lie, Nor a son of man, that He should repent; has He said, and will He not do it? Or has He spoken, and will He not establish it?
- **Psalm 102:27** – But You [O God] are the same, and Your years will not come to an end.
- **Malachi 3:6** – For I, Yahweh, do not change; therefore you, O sons of Jacob, are not consumed.
- **Hebrews 13:8** – Jesus Christ is the same yesterday and today and forever.
- **James 1:17** – Every good thing given and every perfect gift is from above, coming down from the Father of lights, with whom there is no variation or shifting shadow.
- Also see Psalm 33:11, 90:2, 102:25–27, 119:89–90; Isaiah 40:8, 40:28, 44:6; Jeremiah 10:10; 2 Timothy 2:13; Hebrews 6:13–19, 7:24; Revelation 22:13.

2. Why do you think we typically end our prayers with "in the name of Jesus, Amen"?

3. Watch the short film *He Is* — which walks chronologically through the names of Jesus from Genesis through Revelation. It is a profound meditation on our God! As you watch, remember that His names are a picture of who He is—His nature, life, character, reputation, attributes, and identity. And as you behold Him and His names, remember to "hallow" (give reverence and honor) and turn your focus to worship, adoration, and praise—for He is worthy, not merely because of what He does but because of who He is. You can either go to YouTube and search "He Is, Ellerslie" or find the link in the bonus resources at deeperChristian.com/30day.

DAY 05

YAHWEH

Yesterday, we discussed the biblical importance of names and how a name is more than a nomenclature but a revelation of identity, character, nature, reputation, and sometimes even purpose and authority.

With all that in mind, read Psalm 8:1 afresh:

> *O Yahweh, our Lord, how majestic is Your name in all the earth, who displays Your splendor [glory] above the heavens!*

The name of our Lord is majestic!

Hebrews 13:15 reminds us, "Through Him, therefore, let us constantly and at all times offer up to God a sacrifice of praise, which is the fruit of lips that thankfully acknowledge and confess and glorify His name" (AMP).

Not only is the Lord's name majestic, but we are to continually offer the sacrifice of praise to Him, giving thanks unto His name. Why? Because His name is a declaration of His person, presence, identity, and life.

THE NAMES OF GOD

If you watched the *He Is* video yesterday, you heard dozens of God's names all throughout Scripture. While many names are given to Him, there are a few that stand out as distinct:

Yahweh *(LORD, Jehovah)*
Adonai *(Lord, Master)*
Elohim *(God)*
El Elyon *(The Most High God)*
El Olam *(The Everlasting God)*
El Shaddai *(Lord God Almighty)*
Jehovah Jireh *(The Lord Will Provide)*
Jehovah Mekoddishkem *(The Lord Who Sanctifies You)*
Jehovah Nissi *(The Lord My Banner)*
Jehovah Raah *(The Lord My Shepherd)*
Jehovah Rapha *(The Lord That Heals)*
Jehovah Sabaoth *(The Lord of Hosts)*
Jehovah Shalom *(The Lord Is Peace)*
Jehovah Shammah *(The Lord Is There)*
Jehovah Tsidkenu *(The Lord Our Righteousness)*
Qannā *(Jealous)*

We won't be studying each of these names in-depth in this book (though I encourage you to do so at some point), but I want to take time throughout these thirty days to examine a few from this list. You'll soon see that His names are powerful and reveal to us who He is and His involvement in our lives.

YAHWEH
Quick Overview

The name most used throughout Scripture for God is *Yahweh*, used 6,519 times. This name is a bit difficult to nail down as it was the unspeakable name of God. Jews, even to this day, don't pronounce this name; instead, they use a substitute such as Adonai or Hashem (literally meaning "the Name"). In your Bible, sometimes this name is given in all caps in the Old Testament (LORD) and is often pronounced as Yahweh or Jehovah (though we don't know what the original pronunciation was). It is also called the Tetragrammaton for the four letters in this name: YHWH.

Though used throughout the book of Genesis, the significance of Yahweh begins with Moses in the burning bush of Exodus 3.

While speaking to Moses from the bush, God commands Moses to go back to Egypt and free the Israelites from slavery.

> *Then Moses said to God, "Behold, I am about to come to the sons of Israel, and I will say to them, 'The God of your fathers has sent me to you.' And they will say to me, 'What is His name?' What shall I say to them?" And God said to Moses, "I AM WHO I AM"; and He said, "Thus you shall say to the sons of Israel, 'I AM has sent me to you'"* (Exodus 3:14).

What is the name God gives to Moses? YHVH.

In the next verse, God says, "This is **My name forever**,

and this is **My memorial-name** from generation to generation" (Exodus 3:15b).

Interestingly, God's name is merely "I AM." If you or I were to say, "I am," it would beg for something to complete it… "you are what?" we would ask. But for God, the statement is complete—He is "I AM."

It is also important to note that when we talk of God, we don't say "I AM" but rather "HE IS"—the writer of Hebrews picks up on this and says in 11:6, "But without faith it is impossible to please Him, for he who comes to God must believe that **He is**, and that **He is** a rewarder of those who diligently seek Him" (NKJV). We must believe that HE IS (the I AM).

THE GREAT I AM

This unspeakable name has layers of depth in its meaning:

- It conveys that God is Lord and master, the absolute ruler and authority of all things.
- It denotes His omnipotence (He is all-powerful) and supremacy.
- This name also reveals God as eternal and immutable (unchanging). He is, in fact, always the same. His nature does not change. He was, is, and forever will be.

When God says, "I AM," He declares He is who He always will be.

I had you look up a few verses of this amazing truth yesterday, but for the sake of review, listen afresh to a few…

- You are the same… (Psalm 102:27).

- For I, Yahweh, do not change... (Malachi 3:6).
- [God], with whom there is no variation or shifting shadow (James 1:17b).
- Jesus Christ is the same yesterday and today and forever (Hebrews 13:8).

God's nature, character, and identity are always the same!

This truth is significant in our lives because it means when God reveals who He is, we know He is still that way. And perhaps even more noteworthy is the fact that if God cannot change, then we can trust Him. Trust is built over time through consistency of action—so if God is always the same and He cannot change His nature or character, then there is every reason to believe, put our faith in, and cling to Him for life and godliness.

FULFILLED IN JESUS

Every name of God in the Old Testament finds its fulfillment in Jesus. Amazingly, even the name "Jesus" is a compound word comprised of "Yahweh" and the Hebrew verb "to save." Jesus' name means "Yahweh is salvation," or "I AM saves," or "HE IS salvation."

But even more so, Jesus is Yahweh in the flesh. The One who created the heavens and the earth and spoke all things into existence became a man (see Colossians 1:15–16 and John 1:1–4, 14).

Jesus nearly got stoned for saying the same thing. In an argument with the Pharisees, they bring up Abraham as their father. To which Jesus responds, "Truly, truly, I say to you, before Abraham was, I AM" (John 8:58).

This wasn't a casual comment; He was claiming to be God, Yahweh, the great I AM. According to the Jews, this was blasphemy, which is why "they picked up stones to throw at Him, but Jesus hid Himself and went out of the temple" (John 8:59).

A REVELATION OF RELATIONSHIP

What strikes me most about this name is that it's relational. Again, in Exodus 3:15b, God says, "This is My name forever, and this is My memorial-name from generation to generation." This is God's *personal* name. While it bespeaks of His immutability (He doesn't change), it also underscores the relationship He desires to have with His people.

In Exodus 33, we are told that when Moses entered the tent of meeting, "the pillar of cloud would descend and stand at the entrance of the tent; and Yahweh would speak with Moses.... Thus Yahweh used to speak to Moses face to face, just as a man speaks to his friend" (33:9, 11).

The same God who created the universe didn't stand far off; rather, He came near and spoke with Moses like a friend, face to face. We are told the same thing about Abraham (see 2 Chronicles 20:7; Isaiah 41:8; James 2:23), and it's also true about God's desire to have a relationship with you.

Not only have we become the dwelling place of Yahweh (see 1 Corinthians 3:16; 6:19; Ephesians 2:22; Revelation 21:3), but Jesus calls us friends (see John 15:15) and desires to have with us as close of a relationship as He had with the Father (see John 10:14–15; 17:3; 17:20–23).

Doesn't this thought make you stand in awe of Him? I, like David, can only cry out:

> O Yahweh, our Lord, how majestic is Your name in all the earth, who displays Your splendor above the heavens!... What is man that You remember him, and the son of man that You care for him? Yet You have made him a little lower than the angels, and You crown him with glory and majesty!... O Yahweh, our Lord, how majestic is Your name in all the earth! (Psalm 8:1, 4–5, 9).

GO DEEPER

1. Freshly think through what it means to honor and revere God's name, not taking it in vain (see Deuteronomy 5:11).

2. The name Yahweh conveys the idea that God is always the same (He does not change), and therefore, we can fully trust Him. But can *you* honestly say that you fully trust Him? If not, spend time and confess your unbelief and place your complete trust in Him.

3. God wants to form His character in us and make us partakers of His divine nature (see 2 Peter 1:4). This does NOT mean we become gods; instead, we share in His life—He is God, we are not. Interestingly, while we are continually being sanctified (being changed and transformed), we are also called to be "always the same" as Christians. Read this list of how we are told to always

be the same. What areas or aspects do you need to grow in?

> We set the LORD **always** before us: and because He is at our right hand, we shall not be moved (Psalm 16:8). We ought **always** to pray (Luke 18:1), and without ceasing make mention of others **always** in our prayers (Romans 1:9). We thank our God **always** (1 Corinthians 1:4), **always** abounding in the work of the Lord (1 Corinthians 15:58), for He **always** causes us to triumph in Christ (2 Corinthians 2:14). We are **always** bearing about in our bodies the dying of the Lord Jesus, that the life also of Jesus might be made manifest in our body (2 Corinthians 4:10). We are **always** confident (2 Corinthians 5:6), and due to His abounding grace, we **always** have all sufficiency in all things in order to abound to every good work (2 Corinthians 9:8). We are giving thanks **always** for all things (Ephesians 5:20), and **always** making our requests with joy (Philippians 1:4). And we are **always** magnifying Christ in our bodies, whether it be by life, or by death (Philippians 1:20). We are **always** obeying (Philippians 2:12). We are rejoicing in the Lord **always** (Philippians 4:4), praying **always** (Colossians 1:3), and our speech is **always** with grace, seasoned with salt (Colossians 4:6). We are **always** laboring fervently for others in prayer (Colossians 4:12) and giving thanks to God **always** for others (1 Thessalonians 1:2). We **always** follow that which is good (1 Thessalonians 5:15)

and we rejoice **always** (1 Thessalonians 5:16). We are bound to thank God **always** for our brothers and sisters in Christ and we pray **always** (2 Thessalonians 1:3,11; 2 Thessalonians 2:13), making mention of others **always** in our prayers (Philemon 1:4).

DAY 06

ELOHIM

Yesterday, we briefly examined God's intimate and most popular name in Scripture, *Yahweh*. Today, I want to look at another…

Used over 2000 times throughout Scripture, *Elohim* is the first name of God revealed in Scripture. In Genesis 1:1, we are told, "In the beginning, God [Elohim] created the heavens and the earth." Interestingly, *Elohim* appears 35 times between Genesis 1:1–2:3 in the creation account. It is as if God is over-emphasizing the fact He is the Creator of all things.

Let's examine three key aspects of this name.

1. PERSONAL

Elohim isn't a standoffish being who creates a few things and leaves them be. Amazingly, throughout creation, we see God intimately involved in every aspect. When He speaks light into existence, we see Him creating, seeing, separating, and calling (see Genesis 1:3–4). Each of these verbs portrays God involved in His creation.

This is heightened in the creation of humanity when God made male and female in His own image, blessed them, and gave them rule over His creation. In Genesis 2:7, we are told that God's breath is what caused Adam to be a living creature—"Then Yahweh God [Elohim] formed man of dust from the ground and breathed into his nostrils the breath of life; and so the man became a living being."

As you continue throughout Scripture, you find God personally interacting with His creation, even after they rebelled against Him.

Elohim, our God, is personal.

2. PLURAL

The word "Elohim" in Hebrew is plural, coming from the singular word *El* or *Eloah*. And yet, while this word is plural, we know God is singular.

In what is arguably the most popular Old Testament passage to a Jew, called the Shema, Deuteronomy 6:4–5 declares: "Hear, O Israel! Yahweh is our God [Elohim], Yahweh is one! "You shall love Yahweh your God [Elohim] with all your heart and with all your soul and with all your might."

Don't miss the significance here. Moses commands the Israelites to "hear" (the Hebrew word "shema"), meaning not just listen to or hear some sound, but to hear, perceive, understand, and apprehend. And they are to "shema" that Yahweh is our Elohim and that He is ONE.

Though His name is plural, our God is not a multitude of gods; He is one. What a beautiful picture of the Trinity. As Christians, we believe in ONE God with three distinct Persons: Father, Son, and Spirit. While they are each distinct, they are not separate—they are perfectly one. Throughout the centuries, we have labored to understand and give illustrations, and while the Trinity is beyond our comprehension to grasp, the best picture I've heard of is a triangle. In a triangle, each corner is a distinct angle, and yet the angle itself doesn't make it a triangle—it is only when all three distinct angles come together as one that it creates a triangle—three in one. Every illustration breaks down at some point, but that is the best I've heard.

Elohim, our God, is singular; He is one, yet He is plural. Even in the creation account, we see this plural/singular truth—"Then God said, 'Let **Us** make man in **Our** image, according to **Our** likeness...'" (Genesis 1:26a).

What is "hidden in plain sight" in the Old Testament is expounded upon in the New Testament. Jesus explains that "I and the Father are one" (John 10:30) and that He will send us the Holy Spirit, His very Spirit (see John 14:9–31; 16:5–15). The New Testament is strong in affirming that we only have one God, yet in three distinct persons (also see as examples: Matthew 1:23; 3:16–17; 28:19; John 1:1–14; Acts 2:33; 2 Corinthians 1:21–22; Galatians 4:6; Philippians 2:5–8; Colossians 1:15–17; 2:9; 1 Peter 1:1–2; Hebrews 1:1–3).

3. POWERFUL

The name *Elohim* can also be translated as "Judge" or "Strong One." The name bespeaks the greatness of God's power, sovereignty, and authority. He is the Lord over all, and all things have been placed beneath His feet (see Psalm 8:6; 1 Corinthians 15:27; Ephesians 1:22; Hebrews 2:8).

There is no way to measure the immensity or the intensity of God's power. As Martin Lloyd-Jones once wrote in his commentary on Ephesians 1:19, "Take all the dictionaries of the world, exhaust all the vocabularies, and when you have added them all together you have still not begun to describe the greatness of God's power." [5]

Our God, Elohim, spoke everything into existence out of nothing with a mere breath from His lips. "Let there be light," He said, and there was; "Let there be animals," and there were.

I've recently tried my hand at painting. Putting a few squiggles of paint on a canvas takes me hours. Hours to create something from something. And yet our God created everything from nothing in mere moments by a spoken word.

Our God is so powerful that when "the kings of the earth take their stand and the rulers take counsel together against Yahweh and against His Anointed," God merely laughs and holds them in derision (see Psalm 2:1–4). He's not pushed around, manipulated, or coerced; He's the One in control.

OUR PLURAL POWERFUL PERSONAL GOD

Elohim, our Triune God, who is all-powerful and holds the universe in the palm of His hand (see Isaiah 40:12–15), also knows the number of hairs on your head (see Matthew 10:30; Luke 12:7).

The greatness and power of our God doesn't limit His interaction with us; rather, it reveals how much more He desires intimacy with you...yes, YOU. In human society, typically, the more popular and busy someone becomes, the less time they make for the multitudes, and they tend to hide themselves away with a handful. But God is unlike us. He is all-powerful and controls the universe, yet desperately wants an intimate and personal relationship with you. Your circumstance and situation have not escaped His notice. This God who transcends time and space has invaded *your* personal time and space because of His overwhelming love for you (see 1 John 4:8–9; John 3:16).

When we see the name *Elohim*, we are reminded of our Creator, the all-powerful, personal God who came as a man on our behalf. This same "Strong One" took upon Himself humility and humiliation and hung on a blood-soaked beam of wood...so that He could make the way for a relationship with us. And it is this same Jesus who will come again in all His power, for He is still the "Strong One," the Creator of the heavens and earth; Elohim is His name.

Who shall we compare our God to? None. For there is no one in all of heaven or earth that compares to our God. Praise His holy name!

Many, O Yahweh my God, are the wondrous deeds You have done, and Your thoughts toward us; there is none to compare with You. I would declare and speak of them, but they are too numerous to recount (Psalm 40:5).

GO DEEPER

1. Many of us think that Jesus merely "showed up" 2000 years ago, but we forget that He is the Alpha and Omega, the first and the last, the beginning and the end (see Revelation 22:13). Yes, He took on flesh and became a babe 2000 years ago, but He is the Triune God and has always existed. Read these passages about Jesus being the Creator and ponder them in light of what we've talked about Elohim:

- **John 1:1-4** – In the beginning was the Word, and the Word was with God, and the Word was God. He was in the beginning with God. All things came into being through Him, and apart from Him nothing came into being that has come into being. In Him was life, and the life was the Light of men.
- **Romans 11:36** – For from Him and through Him and to Him are all things. To Him be the glory forever. Amen.
- **Ephesians 3:8-9** – To me, the very least of all saints, this grace was given, to proclaim to the Gentiles the good news of the unfathomable riches of Christ, and to bring to light for all what is the administration of the mystery which for ages has been hidden in God who created all things...
- **Colossians 1:15-16** – [Jesus] Who is the image of the invisible God, the firstborn of all creation. For in Him all things were created, both in the heavens and on earth, visible and invisible, whether thrones or dominions or rulers or

authorities—all things have been created through Him and for Him.
- **Hebrews 1:1-2** – God, having spoken long ago to the fathers in the prophets in many portions and in many ways, in these last days spoke to us in His Son, whom He appointed heir of all things, through whom also He made the worlds...
- **Revelation 1:8** – "I am the Alpha and the Omega," says the Lord God, "who is and who was and who is to come, the Almighty."
- **Revelation 3:14** – "And to the angel of the church in Laodicea write: This is what the Amen, the faithful and true Witness, the Beginning of the creation of God..."

2. Spend time with our all-powerful and personal Triune God. Thank Him for His marvelous works and for who He is. Don't ask things from Him; just delight in Him.

DAY 07

SWEETNESS TO THE SOUL

Interspersed between studying God's names (and thus His character, attributes, and nature), we will have practical "adventures" that press us to know Jesus more. David, in Psalm 19:10, reminds us that God's Word is

> *more desirable than gold,*
> *even more than much fine gold;*
> *sweeter also than honey*
> *and the drippings of the honeycomb.*

Most of us come to Scripture with the mindset of duty or obligation rather than delight. Yet David found the Word of God to be a delight, desire, and sweetness to his soul.

How do you see God's Word? Is it with excitement or dread? Obsession or obligation? Delight or duty?

One of the significant shifts in my spiritual life was realizing that when I read God's Word, I'm doing so not to gain information, know the stories, or even check it off a list. I read God's Word to know the Author...reading God's Word is about **relationship**.

Before opening Scripture, remind yourself that you want to dive into His Word because you desire to know Him. Before reading, spend time in communion and prayer, asking God to reset your focus and illuminate His Word so that Jesus is revealed. And be encouraged!—one of the roles of the Holy Spirit, who lives within every believer, is to lead them unto Christ (see John 16:13–14).

Today's Adventure:
Read Colossians.

I love Colossians; it is about the grandeur and glory of Jesus Christ. Before you read this incredible letter, spend time in prayer, then try to read it as if you've never heard it before. Paul is writing to you about Jesus and the lifestyle of a Christian. You know this stuff, but hear it anew.

If you have time (it takes about 15–20 minutes to read it once), you may even want to read it through a couple of times, perhaps in different translations.

Remember, don't read because you have to...like King David, this should be a delight, a desire, and sweetness to your soul.

GO DEEPER

1. If you don't have a love and delight for God's Word, spend some time and honestly answer why. Ask God to remove every motive from your heart besides knowing Him.

2. If you can access an audio Bible, consider listening

to Colossians on repeat for the day. Listen and soak in the book as you find a few spare moments throughout the day.

3. Don't worry about understanding the book's details; try to get the "big picture"/overview by reading it several times.

4. After reading the book several times, how would you describe and summarize Colossians in one sentence?

DAY 08

EXPERIENCE HEARTBURN

Cleopas and another disciple, whom we don't know their name, were walking the seven-mile journey from Jerusalem to a village called Emmaus.

We don't know why they were going there, but we know everything changed when Jesus showed up.

Though they were unable to recognize Him at first, they talked along the way about the Messiah as revealed in the Old Testament—"Then beginning with Moses and with all the prophets,[6] He interpreted [explained] to them the things concerning Himself in all the Scriptures" (Luke 24:27).

As they reached the village, their eyes were opened, and they recognized Jesus. When He vanished from their sight, and before they raced back to Jerusalem to tell the others, they looked at one another and said, "Were not our hearts burning within us while He was speaking to us on the road, while He was opening the Scriptures to us?" (Luke 24:32).

They experienced heartburn.

This is the same kind of heartburn we should

experience when we encounter the Word—both the Written Word (the Bible) and the Living Word (Jesus).

There is something about the Word of God that causes heartburn within believers.

Interestingly, these two disciples experienced heartburn as Jesus revealed Himself through the pages of the *Old Testament*.

All of the Bible is a revelation of Jesus Christ, and He can be seen on every page—whether it be through prophecy (see Isaiah 7:14), symbolism (like the manna in the Wilderness, see John 6:51), or types and shadows (see Romans 5:14; Colossians 2:17; Hebrews 8:5).

Today's Adventure:
Experience heartburn as you discover Jesus in the Old Testament.

Choose one (or several) of the Old Testament passages below and allow the Holy Spirit to reveal the things concerning Jesus in all the Scriptures.

When studying the Old Testament, it is important to remember that the interpretation must be done in the original context and (typically) within a historical/literal sense. Only after establishing the context and understanding of the passage can we investigate and "find" Jesus within the passage. Jumping to conclusions and making things point to Jesus (often out of context) can quickly lead to wrong interpretations and, eventually, twisted doctrines.

For example, every tree in Scripture doesn't point to the cross (though some do), nor whenever the color red is mentioned is it symbolic of the blood—it may just be trees and the color red.

Allow the context (the surrounding passages) to give the primary meaning of a passage, but also allow the Holy Spirit to unveil Jesus to you—for all of Scripture is a revelation of Him.

PASSAGES

Easier
- Psalm 22 (also see Matthew 27:46)
- Exodus 12 (also see 1 Corinthians 5:7 and Hebrews 9:11–10:23)
- Numbers 21:4–9 (also see: John 3:14–18)
- Isaiah 53
- Genesis 3:23–24 (also see: John 14:6; Matthew 7:13–14; John 10:7–9)

A Bit Harder But Profound
- Joshua 3–4
- Psalm 2
- Ruth 1–4
- Exodus 25–27 (The Tabernacle)
- Genesis 28:10–22 (also see: John 1:51)

DAY 09

JEHOVAH JIREH

Yahweh Our Provider

For today's study, I want to tell you three stories.

THE OLD FATHER

After decades of waiting for the promise spoken by God, Abraham, now a hundred years old, saw the promise fulfilled in the birth of his son Isaac. With unspeakable joy, he lavished his boy with everything he'd ever want or need. Life couldn't get better than this.

Yet one day, God spoke again to Abraham and made an unfathomable command: "Take now your son, your only one, whom you love, Isaac, and go forth to the land of Moriah, and offer him there as a burnt offering on one of the mountains of which I will tell you" (Genesis 22:2).

Without wait or complaint, Abraham got up early in the morning and took off with Isaac and two of his servants. Going three days into the Judean hills, Abraham lifted his eyes and saw the place God promised to show him.

Leaving the servants, Abraham took the wood for the sacrifice and laid it upon his son Isaac, himself carrying the knife and fire; they both climbed up the mount. Along the way, Abraham's beloved son looked up and asked innocently, "Dad, I see the fire and wood, but where is the sacrifice?"

As a declaration of faith and trust, Abraham responded: "God will provide for Himself the lamb for a burnt offering, my son."

What heartbreak it must have been for Abraham to bind Isaac and lay him on the altar he built. What trust it must have taken Isaac to lay upon the wood he carried up the hill and watch his father hold a knife over his head.

But when the moment was about to take place, God stayed Abraham's hand and provided the ram in the thicket for the sacrifice.

Abraham went and took the ram and offered it up as a burnt offering instead of his son. And he called the name of that place *Jehovah Jireh*, saying, "Yahweh Will Provide, as it is said this day, 'In the mount of Yahweh it will be provided'" (Genesis 22:14).

THE BELOVED SON

Nearly two thousand years later, another beloved Son was asked to walk up that *same* hill carrying the wood for His own sacrifice.

Just as the beloved son Isaac carried the wood for his sacrifice, so too the cross was placed upon the shoulders of Jesus to carry up the very same mountain Isaac climbed, carrying the wood for His sacrifice.

Winding through the crowded streets, Jesus came to the brow of the hill, a place called Golgotha—on a mount called Moriah, now called Jerusalem. For as it is said, "In the mount of Yahweh it will be provided" (Genesis 22:14). In the past, it was here that God provided a ram in the place of a beloved son. But now it is here that the same God, Jehovah Jireh, provided His beloved Son as the perfect sacrifice to take away the sins of the world.

JEHOVAH JIREH

Though this name only appears once in Scripture (see Genesis 22:14), the fact that God was, is, and always will be a provider is seen throughout the entire Bible.

This name is a compound made up of the name *Yahweh* (Jehovah), which we've talked about on day five, and the word *Jireh (or Yireh),* meaning "to see" or "provision/provides."

In English, the word "provision" is the idea of *pro* (before) and *vision* (to see)—in other words, to see beforehand.

When we say God is Jehovah Jireh, we declare He is the One who sees our needs and supplies or provides what is needed.

There are countless stories throughout Scripture showcasing God as Jehovah Jireh, but let me tell you a quick, modern story.

THE MAN WHO TRUSTED

I love the life of George Müller of Bristol. Throughout his life, he oversaw the care of over 10,000 orphans and never once asked for money for the orphan work or his personal needs; instead, he trusted in the provision of God to supply all they needed.

My favorite story is when Müller was told there was no food for the children one day. As the 300 children entered the dining room before school and sat at their places, Müller did what he always did: he bowed his head and thanked God for providing food. A few minutes after praying, a knock was heard at the door, and a baker stood there and said, "Mr. Müller, I couldn't sleep last night. Somehow, I felt you didn't have bread for breakfast, and the Lord wanted me to send you some. So I got up at 2 a.m. and baked some fresh bread, and have brought it." Müller thanked the baker, and no sooner had he left when there was another knock at the door. This time, a milkman asked if they could use some milk. His milk cart had broken down right in front of the orphanage, and not wanting the milk to spoil and not sure what else to do, he thought maybe it could be of use at the orphanage.[7]

Such stories of faith and provision are all throughout Christian history because our God is the Great Provider, Jehovah Jireh.

GO DEEPER

1. List all the ways God has been a provider in your life. Don't rush it. Write down anything and everything that comes to mind. Spend a few minutes praising God that He is Jehovah Jireh.

2. What areas do you need God to provide in your life

right now? Spend time in prayer and fully place your trust and confidence in our God who provides.

3. Tell someone today about God's goodness and provision in your life. Get creative—use social media, stop a stranger in the streets, write a letter, or call someone.

DAY 10

RENEWING OUR MINDS

Congrats! You've made it a third of the way through the 30-day adventure. I trust you are falling in love with Jesus more each day. Let's dive into today's adventure...

Paul tells us in Ephesians 4:17, "Therefore this I say, and testify in the Lord, that you walk no longer just as the Gentiles also walk, in the futility of their mind..." He goes on to talk about how the world lives in sin and impurity, but that is not how Christians live because, like a coat, we have taken off our former way of living and are now clothed in Christ (see 4:22–24).

We are told in Philippians 2:5 that we are to have the "mind" of Christ (the Greek word, phroneō, is more than just your mental faculties, but your entire orientation of living—your emotions, attitude, focus, and perspective of life).

Isn't it interesting how much of the New Testament is interested in your "mind"? It is to be transformed, guarded, renewed, and there is an entire list in Philippians 4:8 of things we are to set our mind upon.

Paul commands us in Romans 12:2 not to be

conformed to the world but to be transformed by the renewing of our minds. The word "transformed" is the Greek word *metamorphoō,* from which we get the term *metamorphosis*—the transformation process a caterpillar goes through to become a butterfly. Thus, just like a caterpillar transforming into a butterfly, we are to be transformed into a new creature (see 2 Corinthians 5:17) through the renewing of our minds.

Have you noticed how the battle with sin typically begins in the mind? Temptation presents itself and becomes a choice in our mind—deciding whether to walk in life and victory or plunge into sin and destruction.

The Psalmist asks a profound question: "How can a young man keep his way pure?" (Psalm 119:9). While not limited to young men, this is a question every believer must wrestle with—how will we walk in victory and triumph?

The Psalmist answers, "By keeping [guarding] it according to Your word." The Word must guard our lives.

It is not by accident that two verses later, it says, "Your word I have treasured [hidden] in my heart, that I may not sin against You" (119:11).

In a day where we default to smartphones, google, and calculators to do our thinking for us, hiding God's Word in our hearts has often been tossed to the wayside. If I want to look up a verse, I can grab a device and look it up.

But there is something profound when we memorize God's Word—when we hide and treasure it in our lives, the Word never comes back empty. It is powerful, effective, alive, and good for teaching, reproof, correction, and training us in righteousness (see 2 Timothy 3:16; Hebrews 4:12).

If you're like me, you likely have difficulty memorizing Scripture, but I have found tremendous spiritual growth, greater intimacy with Jesus, and a rich blessing when I memorize God's Word—it helps amidst temptation, God brings passages to mind when I teach or talk with others, and often a passage pops in my mind at the moment I need it throughout my day.

And don't worry if you struggle to memorize; this isn't a race—start slow and know plenty of resources are available to help.[8]

Jesus prayed for His disciples that the Father would "sanctify them by the truth; Your word is truth" (John 17:17). Jesus connects our need to be sanctified and made holy with the power of truth in His Word.

We need to be in the Word.

Today's Adventure:
Memorize Philippians 4:8

For an extra challenge, try to memorize 4:4–9.

BONUS TIPS FOR MEMORIZATION

Here are six quick tips and reminders to help you get started.

1. THE AUTHOR LIVES INSIDE

A key to Bible memory is to realize that the Author of Scripture lives inside your life through the indwelling of His Spirit. Though you could memorize Scripture in your ability and wisdom, what if you didn't have to? God wants you to know His Word, and He will enable you to memorize and recall it (which is an excellent reason to always start in prayer).

2. START SLOW

If you haven't memorized much lately, you will find that starting slow will help. Our memory is like a muscle that needs to be exercised and strengthened for optimal performance. Don't start with an entire paragraph; begin with a verse or two and then continue adding more.

3. UNDERSTAND CONTEXT

When you memorize longer passages, knowing the context and flow of what you will be memorizing is helpful. Before you start memorizing, read the passage and surrounding verses (and/or chapters), and even consider reading the entire book several times. I encourage you to read through the passage (and even the book) daily, which will help you memorize faster and ingrain it deeper in your heart and mind. Knowing the flow of thought and the overall context will help you keep things organized as you memorize. If you have time, learn some details about the book itself (for example, if you memorize a passage in Philippians, find out why Paul wrote the book of Philippians, who the Philippians were, where Paul was when he wrote it, etc.).

4. RECITE, READ, LISTEN, QUOTE

Memorizing a single verse is relatively easy, but memorizing longer passages is far more challenging. The key is consistency in your memorization, and having a plan can make things a lot easier:

Give the priority of your memorization time to reviewing old verses. Begin each day's memorization by reviewing the verses you have learned.

Consider memorizing the verse numbers with the passage. This could seem tedious and like a waste of time, but it can help you not forget a verse in a long passage and can help you know exactly where a specific verse is found when you quote it to someone.

Consider memorizing in chunks/paragraphs/sections based on the natural divisions within the passage (i.e., Ephesians 1 could be divided into the following verse sections: 1–2, 3–14, 15–23).

Suggested Daily Procedure:

- Recite the previous day's verse ten times out loud; look at your Bible if you need to.
- Recite all the verses in the passage/book you've memorized.
- Read and say today's (new) verse ten times out loud—it is beneficial to see and hear it simultaneously.
- Quote the new verse ten times out loud without looking.
- Recite the entire memorized passage, including the verse you learned today.

Another Method and Suggestion:

If the above is too intimidating, consider taking one day a week in your devotional time to memorize God's Word. Take a section of Scripture (more than one verse) and read the entire passage aloud several times. Try to quote the passage without looking. Go back and forth until you have the whole passage memorized.

It is important to review this passage throughout the week (not just in the weekly memorization time)—driving, mowing the lawn, etc., are great opportunities to review the memorized passage.

5. REPETITION IS GOOD...OVER TIME

Saying a verse fifty times in one day is good...but not as effective as saying that same verse every day for fifty days. This is a long-term process, so don't pack everything into one day. If you follow the suggested daily procedure above, you will eventually spend most of your memorization time quoting previous verses—which is precisely what you want!

Use "downtime" (and those random five-minute gaps) to recite verses you've memorized throughout your day. Some experts suggest saying a verse every day for 100 days, but whether you recite a verse/passage once a week or every day, it is essential to review and recite it often to keep it in your memory.

6. A FEW MORE FUN (AND HELPFUL) IDEAS

- Write today's verse(s) on an index card so you can keep it with you to look at throughout the

day. Reviewing verses/passages while you drive, wait in line, shower, or brush your teeth is a great way to take advantage of time.
- If you have a problem keeping the words in their correct order, write down the first letter of each word on a card. For example, Philippians 4:8 (NKJV) would be as follows: F, B, WTAT, WTAN, WTAJ, WTAP, WTAL, WTAOGR, ITIAVAITIAP MOTT.
- If you want help with an app, the best one I've found for long-term memorization is "Bible Memory."[9]
- I love to listen to the Bible in my car. Getting an audio Bible with the same translation you use to memorize can help you hear the passage/book differently... and it's a fun challenge to try to quote the verses alongside the audio—it forces you to speak faster than you usually would when reciting the verses.

What are you waiting for? Grab Philippians 4:8 and start today!

Let us strive, every year we live, to become more deeply acquainted with Scripture.
– JC Ryle –

DAY 11

JEHOVAH RAPHA

The God Who Heals

One of my favorite stories in the Old Testament is obscure but incredibly profound.

After escaping slavery in Egypt and walking on dry ground through the Red Sea, the Israelites found themselves three days in the wilderness (a barren desert) without water.

They are at the point of no return.

Their bodies crave liquid, but they have come too far to turn around—to do so would mean death. They have nowhere to go...except to God.

They come to a body of water, but it's undrinkable. The waters are polluted, contaminated, and bitter.

I imagine the first person who saw the glimmer of water on the horizon picked up his pace and rushed to the water's edge with relief and rejoicing. Sticking his hand down into what he presumed would be his salvation from thirst, he spat it back out and gasped in horror that it was nothing more than a façade. It's water all right, but worthless to meet their need.

They called that place Marah (meaning bitter), and

the Israelites, whom scholars tell us were likely around two million in number, complained and murmured against Moses. They cried out, "What shall we drink?"

The Israelites, mere days before, saw the miraculous movement of God in the ten plagues against Egypt. They experienced His provision as He opened the Red Sea and made a way of escape, causing the entire Egyptian army to be destroyed. And yet they now concluded that God led them into the desert to destine them to die of dehydration.

How often, we, too, have lost our focus.

We hear promises such as "I will never desert you, nor will I ever forsake you" (Hebrews 13:5) or "cast all your anxiety on Him, because He cares for you" (1 Peter 5:7), and we nod in agreement but despair in our next breath. How fickle our faith can be.

In their despair and desperation, Moses cried to the Lord, and the passage says, "and Yahweh showed him a tree" (Exodus 15:25).

A tree? Seriously? How is a tree going to fix bitter, polluted waters?

Yet, in trust and faith, Moses threw the tree into the bitter water, and the water wasn't merely made pure…it was made sweet.

Have you ever had water so clean and pure that it tasted sweet? I have, and it's better than any flavor-filled liquid you could offer me.

After giving a command to listen and obey His commands, God makes a profound statement, "for I, Yahweh, am your healer" (Exodus 15:26). Or as another translation says, "For I am the LORD who heals you" (NKJV).

And contained in that statement is another name of our God: *Jehovah Rapha*—the God who heals.

While this is the only place the actual name appears, the Hebrew word *rapha* shows up 67 times throughout the Old Testament.

Strangely, the first time we see the act of healing in Scripture, the word isn't used; stranger still, it is before sin entered the world. After putting Adam into a deep sleep and taking a rib from his body to form Eve, Genesis 2:21 says that God "closed up the flesh at that place." God healed the wound He made in Adam to create the bride.

And as you follow the idea of *rapha* throughout the Old Testament, you see three distinct areas God healed:
- **Physical** (for example: Genesis 20:17; 2 Kings 20:8; Psalm 103:2–5; Jeremiah 30:17)
- **Emotional** (for example: Psalm 147:3)
- **Spiritual** (for example: Psalm 41:4; Jeremiah 3:22)

THE GOD WHO LOVES TO HEAL

But it all led to the point where Yahweh God, our Jehovah Rapha, took on flesh and demonstrated His love for His people.

In Jesus, who is the exact imprint of God's nature (see Hebrews 1:3) and the image of the invisible God (see Colossians 1:15), and in Him dwells the fullness of the Godhead bodily (see Colossians 2:9), we see a God who loves to heal.

The prophet Isaiah, in talking about the coming Messiah, said:

But He was pierced through for our transgressions,

He was crushed for our iniquities; the chastening for our peace fell upon Him, and by His wounds we are healed (Isaiah 53:5).

The Spirit of Lord Yahweh is upon me because Yahweh has anointed me to bring good news to the afflicted; He has sent me to bind up the brokenhearted, to proclaim release to captives and freedom to prisoners... (Isaiah 61:1).

And that's precisely what we see. Jesus preached among the poor, healed the brokenhearted, caused the mute to hear, the blind to see, the lame to leap, the dead to spring to life, and the demons to flee.

Matthew writes, "Jesus was going throughout all Galilee, teaching in their synagogues and preaching the gospel of the kingdom, and healing every kind of disease and every kind of sickness among the people. And the news about Him spread throughout all Syria; and they brought to Him all who were ill, those suffering with various diseases and pains, demoniacs, epileptics, paralytics; and He healed them" (Matthew 4:23–24).

So much so that John records: "many other signs [miracles] Jesus also did in the presence of the disciples, which are not written in this book... And there are also many other things which Jesus did, which if they were written one after the other, I suppose that even the world itself could not contain the books that would be written" (John 20:30, 21:25).

And remember, Jesus is "the same yesterday and today and forever" (Hebrews 13:8).

MORE THAN PHYSICAL?

While I don't want to downplay physical healing, I think it is important to note that while God still heals physically, He appears to have a bigger agenda—spiritual healing.

Whether He decides to heal someone physically or not will be in accordance with what brings Him the most glory.

I know some incredible godly men and women throughout history who dealt with major physical struggles (such as Amy Carmichael, Hudson Taylor, C.T. Studd, David Brainerd, and many others)—yet all of them saw their physical ailments as a wonderful opportunity to showcase God's goodness and glory; and their dependency and faith upon Him deepened.

And it is important to note that even the people Jesus physically healed (even raised from the dead) eventually died.

Again, I don't desire to downplay physical healing—physical healing can be an incredible testimony of God's power and goodness—but it appears God's ultimate plan is not a physical healing but a spiritual one. Jesus guaranteed we would face hardships; Paul encourages us to endure difficulties well... for the sake of the spiritual prize. The reason the early church was willing to face horrific persecution, torture, and painful martyrdom is because they knew who their God was and trusted in His promise of eternal life and a resurrected body.

Even Jesus faced physical and emotional struggles (see Hebrews 4:15; Matthew 26:36–37), which climaxed upon a painful beam of blood-soaked wood... to bring about spiritual healing through the forgiveness of sins and the destruction of the power and authority of sin itself.

HEALING YOUR BITTER WATERS

If you are dealing with a physical struggle or infirmity, I encourage you to surrender yourself afresh to God and ask Him to do with you whichever would give Him the most honor and glory—whether that be complete healing and restoration or the grace and joy to endure the difficulty well.

But all of us have bitter waters in our lives spiritually. The waters of our souls have been polluted, contaminated, and made bitter through sin. It is undrinkable and unusable to the world around us.

What is the solution to the bitter waters? Just as God showed Moses the solution in a tree, we also need a tree in our lives. It's called a cross.

When you allow God to plant the cross of Christ in your life, your bitter waters don't just become clean or even pure…they become sweet. What an amazing foreshadow hidden in the Old Testament.

What our world needs most is *not* a bunch of Christians who live like the world, full of bitter water, under a façade called Christianity. The world needs Christians whose lives have been made pure, clean, and sweet by the power of the cross and able to offer the world something more than talk…something they actually possess and experience.

As Christians, our lives should demonstrate the power of our Great Healer, Jehovah Rapha.

Even in physical infirmity, torture, or difficulty, our lives should reflect our focus and trust in our God. Our churches should showcase the truth that if God could tear down the dividing wall of hostility between the Jews and Gentiles in the early church (see Ephesians 2:11–22), He can still heal any division in His body, the Church, today. Our personal lives should demonstrate His healing power over the work of the flesh and the subtleties of sin. Rather than hide them from view, we should confess, ask forgiveness, and live in the light as He is in the light (see 1 John 1:7). In short, we should live as authentic Christians.

Let us freshly embrace Jesus as Jehovah Rapha, our God who heals us.

GO DEEPER

1. Spend some time quietly before the Lord and allow the Holy Spirit to search your heart, mind, actions, motives, and emotions and see if there is any wicked way (bitter waters) within you (see Psalm 139:23–24). If He brings anything to mind, confess and repent, and begin to walk in obedience to the Word. Allow Him to turn your bitter waters pure and sweet.

2. If you are struggling with why God wouldn't heal every physical or emotional issue or, as an extension, answer every prayer we have with a "yes," I encourage you to listen to my friend Eric Ludy's message called *Two-Sided Ticket* (you can get a link for the sermon at deeperChristian.com/30day).

DAY 11

3. How can God use your life to showcase His life, love, and healing to the world around you? As an "ambassador for reconciliation" (see 2 Corinthians 5:17–21), how do your life and lips declare that He is Jehovah Rapha?

DAY 12

BE LIKE A COW

Joshua 1:8 says, "This book of the law shall not depart from your mouth, but **you shall meditate on it** day and night, so that you may be careful to do according to all that is written in it; for then you will make your way successful, and then you will be prosperous."

While New Age meditation is about emptying your mind, biblical meditation is about placing your mind ON something—an active engagement with God's Word.

Throughout the Bible, we are told to meditate:
- on God's Law (Joshua 1:8)
- on His works (Psalm 77:12)
- on His wonderful works (Psalm 119:27)
- on His precepts (Psalm 119:15)
- on His statutes (Psalm 119:48)
- on His Word / His Promises (Psalm 119:148)
- on the glorious splendor of His majesty (Psalm 145:5)
- on His name (Malachi 3:16)
- and on things that are true, noble, just, pure, lovely, and of good report (Philippians 4:8)

The biblical concept of meditating is to continually

dwell upon, study, ponder, and bring to mind. The picture is of a cow chewing its cud. When a cow eats, it chews, swallows, regurgitates, continues to chew…and repeats the process several times. In a sense, the same should be true of us. We should continually think about the grandness of Jesus Christ, His work upon the Cross, His saving and enabling power, and the depth of His Word. Like a cow, we should "chew" upon truth, swallow it, and then bring it back to mind to ponder and "chew" some more.

Psalm 1 tells us that the one who delights in God's Word and meditates upon it day and night is like a tree planted by streams of water—a tree that doesn't fear what is going on around it (for example, if a drought comes, it has access to limitless water), and as such is immovable and unshakable despite any circumstance.

What an important reminder we each need for the days in which we live.

HOW TO START CHEWING…ERR…MEDITATING

If we want to know Jesus more, we must keep our hearts and minds and focus on Him. We need to meditate upon Him (the Living Word) and His written Word (the Bible) day and night.

Here are a couple of simple steps to get you started chewing:
- **Read** a passage from the Bible.
- **Reflect** upon the passage (in short, find out what it says—ask it questions like a journalist: who, what, when, where, why, how).

- **Remember**—here's the key: you must hold the passage in your mind to ponder it throughout the day. Either memorize the passage or write it on a piece of paper and carry it with you so you can pull it out, look at it, and continue to reflect and ponder it.
- **Respond**—if the Word doesn't take root and transform our lives, what good is it? We need to respond to the truth, applying and obeying the Word through the enabling power of the Holy Spirit.

Today's Adventure:
Meditate (biblically) upon 2 Peter 1:3–8

…seeing that His divine power has granted to us everything pertaining to life and godliness, through the full knowledge of Him who called us by His own glory and excellence. For by these He has granted to us His precious and magnificent promises, so that by them you may become partakers of the divine nature, having escaped the corruption that is in the world by lust. Now for this very reason also, applying all diligence, in your faith supply moral excellence, and in your moral excellence, knowledge, and in your knowledge, self-control, and in your self-control, perseverance, and in your perseverance, godliness, and in your godliness, brotherly kindness, and in your brotherly kindness, love. For if these things are yours and are increasing, they render you neither useless nor unfruitful in the full knowledge of our Lord Jesus Christ (2 Peter 1:3–8).

DAY 12

GO DEEPER

1. Read the following passages to help you better understand the biblical concept of meditation:

- **Joshua 1:8** – "This book of the law shall not depart from your mouth, but you shall meditate on it day and night, so that you may be careful to do according to all that is written in it; for then you will make your way successful, and then you will be prosperous."
- **Psalm 1:2–3** – But his delight is in the law of Yahweh, and in His law he meditates day and night. And he will be like a tree firmly planted by streams of water, which yields its fruit in its season and its leaf does not wither; and in whatever he does, he prospers.
- **Psalm 19:14** – Let the words of my mouth and the meditation of my heart be acceptable in Your sight, O Yahweh, my rock and my Redeemer.
- **Psalm 104:34** – Let my musing [meditation] be pleasing to Him; as for me, I shall be glad in Yahweh.
- **Psalm 143:5–6** – I remember the days of old; I meditate on all You have done; I muse on the work of Your hands. I stretch out my hands to You; my soul reaches for You like a weary land. Selah.
- **Isaiah 26:3** – "The steadfast of mind You will keep in perfect peace because he trusts in You.
- **Philippians 4:8** – Finally, brothers, whatever is true, whatever is dignified, whatever is right, whatever is pure, whatever is lovely, whatever is

commendable, if there is any excellence and if anything worthy of praise, consider these things.
- Also, consider reading Psalm 77:12; 145:5; Malachi 3:16; and Psalm 119.

2. Spend time in prayer and ask God to help you set your mind on His Word and for His truth to be the meditation of your heart day and night.

DAY 13

JEHOVAH SHALOM

Yahweh is our Peace

"Shalom, shalom."

Those words always bring a smile to my face.

Every time I lead a trip to Israel[10] to study the Bible on location, I can't help but smile at the friendly greeting our Hebrew guide and my friend, Dan, pronounces on the bus each morning. As we make our way through the Holy Land and I open my Bible to teach, the underlying desire is for every person on the trip to experience the shalom of God.

Shalom. Peace.

While it is the standard greeting of Israelites past and present, this word means far more than what we typically think of as "peace."

I hear "peace" and think of sitting on a beach under a warm sun, holding a cup of cold sweet tea, enjoying the sound of crashing waves, with a good book in hand.

The New Oxford American Dictionary defines *peace* as: "freedom from disturbance; tranquility; a state in which there is no war."[11]

That is all true but fails to get at the Hebrew understanding.

Shalom contains the idea of removing hostility (a rest from war), but the word can also mean well-being, health, prosperity, security, soundness, goodness, friendship, salvation, completeness, and wholeness.

When I greet an Israeli, and we say "shalom" to each other, it declares there is no hostility between us, and it is also a blessing that we would each experience good health, well-being, and an incredible day in the Lord.

"Shalom, shalom," then, would be a double blessing of such.

FINDING PEACE

Used over 200 times in the Old Testament and 95 times in the New, true peace is not found in the circumstances surrounding us but in the One who *is* our peace, Jesus Christ.

Paul boldly declares, "He [Jesus] is our peace…" (Ephesians 2:14).

One of the significant shifts in my spiritual life came when I realized that when God wants to give us something, He doesn't give us the *thing*; He gives us Jesus. In one of my favorite passages, 2 Peter 1:3, Peter reminds us that everything we need for life and godliness is found in one single place: Jesus.

When I ask God for joy, He doesn't give me a pill called "joy," nor does He change the circumstances I'm in; He gives me Himself—"In [His] presence is fullness of joy; in [His] right hand there are pleasures forever" (Psalm 16:11). Jesus becomes my joy.

When I plead for God's love to showcase itself in my life, I don't get a bottle of love to drink; I get the One who is love itself (see 1 John 4:8, 16).

When we look at the Fruits of the Spirit in Galatians 5:22–23, they are all fruits of... *the Spirit*. These attributes will naturally come out of our lives when the Spirit resides within us. They are simply the characteristics of Jesus that the Spirit wants to produce in and through us.

So, if you need love, joy, peace, patience, kindness, goodness, faithfulness, gentleness, or self-control, don't try to grit your teeth and self-produce them. Sure, you might be able to generate a little patience or kindness, but the actual life of Christ can only be produced by the Spirit of Christ living within you.

Everything you need for life and godliness is found in Jesus Christ.

We desperately need Jesus.

Which brings us back to peace. Shalom.

You won't find peace in your circumstances; you experience it in Christ.

Hostility and hardship may bully us from the outside; however, we can still experience inner peace and freedom from that hostility when we find our refuge in Him (see Psalm 17:7; 18:2; 18:30; 28:8; 31:2).

Jesus encourages us, "Peace I leave with you; My peace I give to you; not as the world gives do I give to you. Do not let your heart be troubled, nor let it be fearful" (John 14:27). What is the peace He is leaving? It is not something; it is Someone—His Holy Spirit, the Spirit of peace (see John 14:26).

Where is peace found? In Christ alone.

If we seek peace in our circumstances, we may find

momentary relief during good times but will be sadly disappointed during difficulty. True peace is a Person named Jesus—who is constant during good times and bad (see Hebrews 13:8).

Peace isn't a feeling as much as it is a position of living. Even amidst the bomb blasts of life, you can experience peace because, as Christians, our position is IN CHRIST, and He is our peace. Perhaps you could say that peace is a byproduct of being in Jesus. I don't go to Jesus to obtain peace (to get something from Him); instead, when I pursue Jesus for intimacy and relationship with Him, I quickly discover that peace becomes evident in my life. So don't seek after the peace; seek after the Prince of Peace (see Isaiah 9:6).

JEHOVAH SHALOM

One time in Scripture, God is given the name *Jehovah Shalom* (The Lord is Peace).

After calling Gideon to rescue the Israelites from the hands of Midian, Gideon offers a sacrifice to God and cries out, "Alas, O Lord Yahweh! For now I have seen the angel of Yahweh face to face." Judges 6:22-24 goes on to say: "And Yahweh said to him, 'Peace to you. Do not fear; you shall not die.' So Gideon built an altar there to Yahweh and named it Yahweh is Peace. To this day it is still in Ophrah of the Abiezrites."

Gideon recognized that the peace God promised wasn't found in the circumstances but in God alone. Gideon took God's declaration of "Peace to you. Do not fear," turned it around, and called the place *Yahweh is Peace!*

What if we did that in our lives?

We've been given more than a promise of peace; we've received the Prince of Peace Himself. If Jesus is indeed our peace and lives within us via the Holy Spirit, shouldn't our thoughts, words, and actions declare that God continues to be Jehovah Shalom? When the world looks at our lives, shouldn't they see the evidence of shalom within us because He indwells us?

May we live in this day and age, declaring with our lives and lips that Jesus doesn't merely give us peace; He is our peace.

GO DEEPER

1. Scholar Joshua M. Greever states, "In the Old Testament, the term 'peace' is often used to describe a relationship characterized by friendship, care, loyalty, and love."[12] How does this give you further insight into the truth of what it means for Jesus to be our peace?

2. Several times in Scripture, when an individual encounters God, the location is renamed for the event or the character of God (see Genesis 16:6–7; 33:20; 35:7; Exodus 17:15). Consider this in light of the fact that when we encounter God and place our faith in Him, we are given the new name "Christian," we become a living sacrifice (see Romans 12:1–2), and now we are to bear His life and character.

3. Read this quote by Warren Wiersbe and ask God to speak to you through it.

DAY 13

There is always "joy and peace in believing" (Romans 15:13), but unbelief brings fear and worry. God had to give Gideon a message of peace to prepare him for fighting a war. Unless we're at peace with God, we can't face the enemy with confidence and fight the Lord's battles.... Gideon now believed the Lord was able to use him, not because of who he was but because of who God was. Whenever God calls us to a task that we think is beyond us, we must be careful to look to God and not to ourselves. "Is anything too hard for the Lord?" God asked Abraham (Genesis 18:14); and the answer comes, "For with God nothing shall be impossible" (Luke 1:37). Job discovered that God could do everything (Job 42:2), and Jeremiah admitted that there was nothing too hard for God (Jeremiah 32:17). Jesus told His disciples, "With God all things are possible" (Matthew 19:26); and Paul testified, "I can do all things through Christ who strengthens me" (Philippians 4:13, NKJV).[13]

4. Examine your prayer life. How often do you ask for things FROM Jesus rather than asking for more of Him? If He is all you need for life and godliness (see 2 Peter 1:3), how should that affect your praying, speaking, and living? Spend time with Him today and delight in the fact He Himself is your peace (see Ephesians 2:14; Malachi 5:5; Romans 15:33; Isaiah 9:6).

DAY 14

I RAISE MY EBENEZER

In the classic hymn, "Come Thou Fount of Every Blessing," the second verse begins, "Here I raise my Ebenezer…"

Obviously, it is not referring to the main character, Ebenezer Scrooge, in Dickens' *Christmas Carol*.

The song is harkening back to 1 Samuel 7:12, "Then Samuel took a stone and set it between Mizpah and Shen, and he named it Ebenezer. And he said, 'Thus far Yahweh has helped us.'"

As a reminder of the great victory God gave Israel over the Philistines, Samuel erected a stone and called it Ebenezer, literally meaning "stone of help." It was a stone of remembrance, a memorial, and a testimony of God's help and provision during times of trouble.

A similar thing happened years before when Joshua led the Israelites across the Jordan to enter the Promised Land. After crossing, Joshua had each tribe choose a stone and set it up as a memorial to all generations of God's faithfulness and provision (see Joshua 4:1–9).

Remembering something is to purposefully keep it in our mind, preserve its memory, and be able to recall it.

We each need stones of remembrance in our lives.

It may not be actual rocks, but we need something to bring our God's greatness, generosity, glory, and grandeur to mind.

How often have you said, "I'll always remember this moment" or "I'll never forget how God provided in my desperate need," only to find yourself forgetting it days or weeks later?

I was recently talking to a missionary friend of mine, and he said that the greatest honor a missionary receives is having their photo on someone's fridge—because they know it will be a physical reminder for the family to pray for the missionary, the native people, and the Gospel work in that country. Their photo becomes an Ebenezer, a physical reminder to think about the missionary and pray.

We all need to create stones of remembrance—an Ebenezer—to "remember the deeds of Yahweh; surely I will remember Your wonders of old. I will meditate on all Your work and muse on Your deeds. O God, Your way is holy; what god is great like God?" (Psalm 77:11–13).

Today's Adventure:

Make a list of 5–10 things God has done or provided for you, your family, or your church that you don't want to forget. Find a way to memorialize them—for example, journal about each event, create an artistic representation to hang on your wall, or find a stone and write the event on it and literally begin your own "pile of stones."

The method of remembering is less important than actually remembering. Still, I would encourage you to find a time regularly (monthly, yearly, etc.) when you read back through and bring to mind the works of God. The reminder is important to build your faith that the same God who provided in the past is the same God who can provide in the present, and it is a fresh reminder to trust in His faithfulness and to worship Him for Who He is and all He has done.

And while we may poetically sing of raising our Ebenezer, may we always remember that He is the fount of many blessings, for great is His faithfulness.

GO DEEPER

Share your "stones of remembrance" with the people around you. Remind yourself and others of God's faithfulness, goodness, love, and provision.

DAY 15

EL OLAM

The Everlasting God

The observable universe is estimated to be 93 billion light-years in diameter (one light-year is 5.88 trillion miles).

If I may continue with this little science side-track, light travels at the speed of 186,282 miles per second (or, for my international friends, 299,792 kilometers per second). Which means...

- In one second, light can travel around the entire planet 7.5 times.
- It takes 1.3 seconds for light to go from the earth to the moon.
- To go from the sun to earth, light takes 8 minutes.
- The nearest star system to us is Alpha Centauri, which takes light 4.3 years to get to.
- If you wanted to go across our Milky Way Galaxy (the galaxy we live in), from one end to the other, some estimate it would take between 100,000 and 200,000 years at the speed of light.
- The closest minor galaxy to us (the Canis Major Dwarf Galaxy) is 25,000 light years away. And

the closest major galaxy (the Andromeda Galaxy) is a mere 2.5 million light-years away. That's the closest! And yet, there are reportedly between 200 billion and 2 trillion galaxies in the observable universe.

I don't know about you, but hearing such numbers boggles the mind.

Considering that human history is around 6,000 years old, if Adam left the day God created him, traveling at the speed of light, he'd still only be a quarter of the way to the constellation Hercules (which is in our galaxy).

Our Great God

Despite the vastness of the universe, all of creation was spoken into existence by our great God.

Isaiah 40:12, speaking of the greatness of our God, uses symbolic language to describe how much bigger God is than anything we can fathom in His creation, "Who has measured the waters in the hollow of His hand, and encompassed the heavens by the span, and calculated the dust of the earth by the measure, and weighed the mountains in a balance and the hills in a pair of scales?"

The word "span" Isaiah uses to speak of measuring the universe (the heavens) is the width of a hand. In other words, Isaiah uses symbolic language to say that God is so great and immense that even the universe (all 200+ billion galaxies) can fit within the palm of His hand.

We have a great God, indeed.

Isaiah goes on to say, "Do you not know? Have you not heard? The Everlasting God, Yahweh, the Creator of the ends of the earth, Does not become weary or tired. His understanding is unsearchable" (Isaiah 40:28).

FROM EVERLASTING TO EVERLASTING

One of God's names is *El Olam*, often translated as The Everlasting God.

Olam is a word that can mean everlasting, ancient, lasting, or constancy; it is sometimes understood to refer to the world, universe, or everlasting time or space.

El Olam, much like the name *Yahweh*, speaks of God's sovereignty, authority, and immutability (He doesn't change). But *El Olam* also gives the concept that God is the eternal ruler of the entire universe and who is beyond time or space, without a beginning or end (also see: 1 Peter 1:20; Hebrews 7:3; Revelation 1:8; 21:6; 22:13).

God is the Eternal, Everlasting God. He is El Olam.

Moses declares in Psalm 90:2, "Before the mountains were born or You brought forth the earth and the world, even from **everlasting** to **everlasting**, You are God." From *olam* to *olam*, He is God.

Moses reminded the Israelites what God did for them when he said, "The eternal God is a dwelling place, and underneath are the everlasting arms; and He drove out the enemy from before you, and said, 'Destroy!' So Israel dwells in security, the fountain of Jacob secluded, in a land of grain and new wine; His heavens also drop down dew. Blessed are you, O Israel; who is like you, a people saved by Yahweh, who is the shield of your help and the sword of your majesty! So your enemies will cower before you, and you will tread upon their high places" (Deuteronomy 33:27–29).

Isaiah wrote, "Trust in Yahweh forever, for in Yah—Yahweh Himself—we have an everlasting [olam] Rock" (Isaiah 26:4).

Jeremiah said, "But Yahweh is the true God; He is the living God and the everlasting King..." (Jeremiah 10:10).

Our God is eternal, everlasting, enduring, unchanging, the God of Ages, the One who spoke the universe into existence and yet can measure it in the hollow of His hand. He is above all and has authority over all things. He is the living King of kings for all eternity.

UNDER A TAMARISK TREE

Though Scripture speaks of God being *olam*, there is only one time the actual name *El Olam* is used—Genesis 21:33. *For note, Isaiah does use the term "Everlasting God" in Isaiah 40:28, but it is a slightly different construction and speaks of God's perpetuity or the fact He is everlasting, without end (in essence, the same concept, but not used as a specific name).*

At the end of Genesis 21, Abraham makes a covenant with Abimelech in Beersheba (the southern part of the Promised Land). After Abimelech departs, Abraham "planted a tamarisk tree at Beersheba, and there he called upon the name of Yahweh, the Everlasting God" (Genesis 21:33).

It's important to note that nomads, like Abraham, typically don't plant trees. Even today, nomads who wander around with their herds and flocks don't spend enough time in one place for a tree to grow and mature, so they don't plan them.

To plant a tree means investing in a location for future generations. In this case, Abraham establishes a memorial to declare that God is El Olam, the Everlasting God. To proclaim that God rules and reigns for the long term (eternity), Abraham plants a symbol for the long term, a tree that takes years to mature.

While Abraham spent much of his life elsewhere, this tamarisk tree—a tree with many branches and small leaves, growing to a height of twenty to thirty feet—was a sign for future generations that God is everlasting, He is in control, and they could trust Him just as Abraham did.

I don't think it is by accident that God calls Abraham to sacrifice Isaac in Genesis 22. Immediately after Abraham declares God to be El Olam, the Everlasting God, God tests Abraham's faith and trust.

The writer of Hebrews says, "By faith Abraham, when he was tested, offered up Isaac, and he who had received the promises was offering up his only son, to whom it was said, 'In Isaac your seed shall be called.' He considered that God is able to raise people even from the dead, from which, figuratively speaking, he also received him back" (Hebrews 11:17–19).

The test proved that God is the provider (Jehovah Jireh, see Genesis 22:14) and that Abraham truly believed God to be El Olam.

I love the thought that God is the God of the "long term." He doesn't grow weary or faint. He's in it till "the end"—though in God's case, there is no end, for He is eternal and everlasting.

"Do you not know? Have you not heard? The Everlasting God, Yahweh, the Creator of the ends of the earth, does not become weary or tired. His understanding is unsearchable" (Isaiah 40:28).

Paul told Timothy, "Now to the King of the ages, immortal, invisible, the only God, be honor and glory forever and ever. Amen" (1 Timothy 1:17).

May our lives reflect that God is El Olam, worthy of all honor, glory, and praise forever and ever.

GO DEEPER

1. Since Jesus is the fulfillment of every name of God, including El Olam, how does knowing that practically change your life? Consider your answer in light of what author Elmer Towns says:

> *By calling on God as El Olam, Abraham was calling on the One Who is always and eternally available to us.... People today need just such a God as the eternal, unchangeable Lord, El Olam. We call on Him because "thy tender mercies and thy lovingkindnesses...have been ever [olam] of old" (Psalm 25:6). David also said that "the LORD is good; his mercy is everlasting; and His truth endureth to all generations" (100:5). El Olam means "the mercy of the LORD is from everlasting to everlasting upon them that fear him, and his righteousness unto children's children" (103:17).*[14]

2. Read Isaiah 26:4—*"Trust in Yahweh forever, for in Yah—Yahweh Himself—we have an everlasting Rock."* Isaiah says that God is an "everlasting [olam] rock." It is interesting that while a tree is symbolic of longevity, a rock is even more so. A tree may live for thousands of years, but a rock endures "forever." How does this concept help you understand that El Olam is our rock, fortress, and security? Consider reading: Deuteronomy 32:4; 2 Samuel 22:32; Psalm 18:2; 18:31; 31:3; 62:1–2; 95:1; 1 Corinthians 10:4; 1 Peter 2:4–6.

3. Examine your faith and trust in God. Can you proclaim Him as El Olam? Consider spending extended time with our Everlasting God today and delight in the fact He is the King of the ages, immortal, invisible, the only God, to whom belongs all honor and glory forever and ever. Amen.

DAY 16

LORD, TEACH US TO PRAY

As the disciples finished watching Jesus spend time in prayer with the Father, they asked Him, "Lord, teach us to pray" (Luke 11:1b).

Isn't it interesting that the disciples never asked Jesus how to do miracles, cast our demons, or communicate effectively—yet they asked Jesus to teach them how to pray. The communion, intimacy, and connection Jesus had with the Father was so rich and powerful that the disciples wanted in on it.

Jesus not only taught His disciples how to pray (see Luke 11:2-13 and Matthew 6:5-15), but He also prayed that the same kind of intimacy He had with the Father would be the same intimacy they would have with Him (see John 17:20-26).

For many of us, prayer is giving our wishlist to God—it is talking *at* God. But prayer is relational, and one of the great lessons in the school of prayer is listening. Prayer should be a fellowship and communication between you and God, which means you need to listen, not just talk. Remember the illustration from when we were children: you have two ears and only one mouth—so too, we should listen more than we speak, especially in prayer.

For others, prayer is merely our routine before meals or bedtime, yet prayer must move beyond habit. E.M. Bounds rightly said…

> *"Prayer ought to enter into the spiritual disciplines, but it ceases to be prayer when it is carried on by habit only.… Desire gives fervor to prayer. The soul cannot be listless when some great desire fixes and inflames it… Strong desires make strong prayers… The neglect of prayer is the fearful token of dead spiritual desires. The soul has turned away from God when desire after Him no longer presses it into the closet."*[15]

When prayer becomes about communion and intimacy with the Living God, we will know Him more deeply, and that fervent and believing prayer lays the foundation for holiness. D.L. Moody is known to have said that prayer will either keep you from sin or sin will keep you from prayer *(note: it is also attributed to him that he said the same thing about spending time in God's Word)*.

Leonard Ravenhill said it his way: "A sinning man will stop praying, and a praying man will stop sinning."[16] He also said:

> *No man is greater than his prayer life.… Poverty-stricken as the Church is today in many things, she is most stricken here, in the place of prayer. We*

have many organizers, but few agonizers; many players and payers, few pray-ers; many singers, few clingers; lots of pastors, few wrestlers; many fears, few tears; much fashion, little passion; many interferers, few intercessors; many writers, but few fighters. Failing here, we fail everywhere. The two prerequisites to successful Christian living are vision and passion, both of which are born in and maintained by prayer.[17]

If you need a good reminder about prayer, speak to Jesus like speaking to a good friend. When we talk with a close friend, we don't worry about how much time has passed or what to say; we talk and enjoy the conversation. It is usually only when we speak with a stranger that we fidget, look at our watches, and see how fast we can get on with our lives.

If you need a few other suggestions:
1. I encourage you to spend the first few minutes **meditating** (yes, like a cow—see day 12) on the greatness and grandeur of Christ. Ponder His character and nature, reflect upon His goodness and marvelous deeds, consider what Scripture says about Him, and turn that into worship and adoration to Him. Come to Him and just delight in Who He is! (see Psalm 63:3–4; 145:10; Hebrews 13:15).
2. **Remember to listen** (see Psalm 37:7; 46:10; 81:11–13).
3. **Confess your sin.** Sin hinders our relationship with God, so as we come to Him in prayer, allow

His Spirit to search your heart and mind and reveal anything you need to repent of and turn away from (see Psalm 139:23–24; 1 John 1:9; Psalm 66:18; Daniel 9:20).
4. **Be thankful** for what God has done in the past, what He is doing in the present, and what He promises to do in the future (see Philippians 4:6; Colossians 3:17; 1 Thessalonians 5:18; Psalm 34:1).
5. **Don't be self-focused**. So often, our prayers become all about "me me me." While it is not wrong to bring your personal needs and requests before God, let God give you a heart and burden for others. Pray for your spouse, family, friends, church (and especially your pastor), community, the government and its leaders, missionaries and ministries, the persecuted church, pray for revival, unsaved friends and acquaintances, etc.

Today's Adventure:
Pray. Don't worry about the length of time, and enjoy the intimacy, fellowship, and communion with your best friend, Jesus.

GO DEEPER

Consider these quotes and how you can take the concepts mentioned and apply them practically to your prayer life.

- "When one fails to pray, one fails to trust God. When one fails to trust God, he fails to exercise

faith. Whatever is not of faith the Bible calls sin. When we fail to trust God by failing to pray, we doubt His sovereignty and question His goodness." (Unknown)
- "God does nothing but in answer to prayer." (John Wesley)[18]
- "To pray is to change! Prayer is the central avenue God uses to transform us. If we are unwilling to change we will abandon prayer as a noticeable characteristic in our lives." (Richard Foster)[19]
- "Prayer—secret, fervent, believing prayer—lies at the root of all personal godliness." (William Carey)[20]
- "I have been helped…by praying for others; for by making an errand to God for them, I have gotten something for myself." (Samuel Rutherford)[21]
- "Only turning God's house into a house of fervent prayer will reverse the power of evil so evident in the world today." (Jim Cymbala)[22]
- "You must pray with all your might. That does not mean saying your prayers, or sitting gazing about in church or chapel with eyes wide open while someone else says them for you. It means fervent, effectual, untiring wrestling with God…This kind of prayer, be sure, the devil and the world and your own indolent, unbelieving nature will oppose. They will pour water on this flame." (William Booth)[23]
- "People do not drift toward holiness. Apart from grace-driven effort, people do not gravitate toward godliness, prayer, obedience to Scripture, faith, and delight in the Lord. We drift toward

compromise and call it tolerance; we drift toward disobedience and call it freedom; we drift toward superstition and call it faith. We cherish the indiscipline of lost self-control and call it relaxation; we slouch toward prayerlessness and delude ourselves into thinking we have escaped legalism; we slide toward godlessness and convince ourselves we have been liberated." (D.A. Carson)[24]

- "Prevailing prayer can be exhausting work. Many Christians are so spiritually frail, sickly, and lacking in spiritual vitality that they cannot stick to prayer for more than a few minutes at a time. Such people are too spiritually weak to know how to pray with real soul travail." (Wesley L. Duewel) [25]
- "Prayer is not getting things from God, that is the most initial stage; prayer is getting into perfect communion with God." (Oswald Chambers)[26]

DAY 17

JEHOVAH RAAH + ADONAI

Yahweh My Shepherd + Master

Yahweh is my shepherd; I shall not want.
Often quoted during difficulty, trials, and funerals, the encouragement of God leading us without fear through "the valley of the shadow of death" is hope-filled and a balm to the cacophony of chaos that may surround us.

JEHOVAH RAAH

In Psalm 23, we find another of God's names—Jehovah Raah, The LORD (Yahweh) my Shepherd.

What I love about this name in Psalm 23 is that David does not use a noun to describe God as "shepherd" but instead uses a verb (actually a participle), which gives the idea of "actively shepherding." The emphasis is that it shows God as intimately and actively doing the work of a shepherd. He is not only called "Shepherd," He actually *is* a shepherd and *is* caring for His sheep right now.

DAY 17

Throughout Scripture, God is often described as a shepherd over His flock, the people of Israel.

- Then Moses spoke to Yahweh, saying, "May Yahweh, the God of the spirits of all flesh, appoint a man over the congregation, who will go out and come in before them, and who will lead them out and bring them in, so that the congregation of Yahweh will not be like sheep which have no shepherd" (Numbers 27:15–17).
- Then David spoke to Yahweh when he saw the angel who was striking down the people, and said, "Behold, it is I who have sinned, and it is I who have done unrighteousness; but these sheep, what have they done? Please let Your hand be against me and my father's house" (2 Samuel 24:17).
- You led Your people like a flock by the hand of Moses and Aaron (Psalm 77:20).
- But He led forth His own people like sheep and guided them in the wilderness like a flock…(Psalm 78:52).
- But as for us, as Your people and the sheep of Your pasture, we will give thanks to You forever; from generation to generation we will recount Your praise (Psalm 79:13).
- O Shepherd of Israel, give ear, You who guide Joseph like a flock…(Psalm 80:1).
- Know that Yahweh, He is God; it is He who has made us, and not we ourselves; we are His people and the sheep of His pasture (Psalm 100:3).
- Also see: Psalm 74:1; Jeremiah 23:1–4; Ezekiel 34; Matthew 15:24

THE WORK OF A SHEPHERD

Much is written on the life of a shepherd, and I mention a few resources in the Go Deeper section if you want to study more. But I want to highlight a few aspects of this Psalm.

I've outlined the Psalm in four sections:
    Verse 1   Premise
    Verse 2–3   Provision
    Verse 4–5   Protection
    Verse 6   Purpose

In verse one, David lays forth the premise of the entire psalm, from which everything else flows. The whole focus of Psalm 23 is not upon the sheep but on the Shepherd. And the reason "I shall not want" or "I do not lack" is because Yahweh is actively shepherding me. When I humble myself and allow myself to be shepherded, I find I have everything I need for life and godliness (see 2 Peter 1:3).

The entire purpose, David concludes in verse six, is that I realize "goodness and lovingkindness [the Hebrew word "hesed"[27]] will pursue me all the days of my life, and I will dwell in the house of Yahweh forever." David declares that the point and redemptive purpose of all the Shepherd does in our lives (verses two through five, showing why we "do not lack") is to experience the Shepherd's goodness and lovingkindness and to dwell intimately in His presence forever.

As you study the lives of ancient shepherds, you find they had three critical roles concerning their sheep:

1. PROTECTION

A shepherd protected the sheep. The rod and staff of the shepherd not only gave guidance and comfort to the sheep but were also used to ward off animals and bandits who hoped to steal them. Shepherds were willing to put their lives at risk, even lay down their lives for the sake of their sheep.

2. PROVISION

A shepherd gave up his comforts and pleasures to provide for the sheep. In Israel, sheep were grazed near the desert with few shrubs and pastures. A shepherd knew where to find the "green pastures" and lead the sheep near still waters. He was attentive to the sheep when they needed rest or when he needed to push them over the next hill to find provision.

3. DIRECTION

A shepherd gave directions to his sheep. Sheep are foolish animals and the only animal I know of in God's kingdom that demands a shepherd. You will never find a wild flock of sheep anywhere in the world because sheep require someone to lead, protect, and provide for them. With the guttural call of his voice, the light taps of his rod and staff, and the relationship he developed with his sheep, a shepherd would lead and direct his sheep to where they needed to go.

OUR GOOD SHEPHERD

It's not by accident that *we* are called God's sheep. Just as sheep require a shepherd, so do we.

John 10 has become one of my favorite chapters in the Bible. In this chapter, Jesus gives two of His "I AM" statements—"I AM the Gate of the sheep" (10:7) and "I AM the Good Shepherd" (10:11, 14).

The word "good" in Greek has a breadth of meanings: beautiful, handsome, excellent, eminent, choice, surpassing, precious, useful, suitable, commendable, or admirable. And it also gives the idea of being genuine and approved. In this context, it also suggests competence and ability. In other words, Jesus isn't merely a "good" shepherd; He is the most excellent, surpassing, precious, useful, and suitable shepherd who is also genuine, approved, competent, and able to do the work of a shepherd.

He isn't faking it. He isn't just trying His hand at a new job. He is the most superior shepherd. He is our Good Shepherd!

In John 10, Jesus used the picture of His sheep gathered in a pen or near a waterhole, mixed with other flocks of sheep. How does a shepherd separate his flock from someone else's? Jesus says, "The sheep hear his voice, and he calls his own sheep by name and leads them out. When he brings all his own out, he goes ahead of them, and the sheep follow him because they know his voice." (10:3–4).

The guttural call of each shepherd is different; hence, as a shepherd begins to walk away from the pen or waterhole, he calls his sheep, and they know the shepherd's voice so well they follow. What if we did that with Jesus? What if we knew His voice so well that we were quick to obey and follow?

Jesus continued, saying, "I am the good shepherd; the good shepherd lays down His life for the sheep.... I am the good shepherd, and I know My own and My own know Me, even as the Father knows Me and I know the Father; and I lay down My life for the sheep. And I have other sheep, which are not from this fold; I must bring them also, and they will hear My voice; and they will become one flock with one shepherd.... My sheep hear My voice, and I know them, and they follow Me..." (John 10:11, 14–16, 27).

What is Jesus doing in our lives? He is our Good Shepherd who gives protection, provision, and direction.

Isn't it fascinating that those are typically the three things we pray about most? Examine your prayer life, and you'll likely find that most of your praying falls into one of those three categories. Yet, as a Good Shepherd, Jesus will shepherd you and provide protection, provision, and direction in your life.

OUR GREAT MASTER

Another of God's names is *Adonai* (in the Old Testament) or *Kurios* (in the New Testament), often translated as *Lord* or *Master*. In Bible times, a master was required by law to provide three things for his slaves: protection, provision, and direction.

Paul often referred to himself as a "slave of Christ." A servant was usually paid and had a choice of whether they worked; a slave had no such choice nor pay—a slave fully submitted to and came under the authority of their master.

Interestingly, the New Testament uses the term *Lord* (*kurios*) for Jesus 720 times, but the term *savior* only 24. As my good friend Dan McConnaughey has said, "We love and prefer Jesus as savior, though for eternity He is Lord and Master."

Yes, Jesus is our savior! But He is also our Lord and Master. We must, therefore, humble ourselves and come under His authority. When we do, we discover that as our Lord and Good Shepherd, Jesus will supply protection, provision, and direction in our lives.

Yet remember, as both Lord and Shepherd, He doesn't stand aloof, distantly gazing upon us and watching what we do, ready to slap our hand; rather, the titles *Shepherd* and *Lord* denote a relationship. Jesus says, "I am the good shepherd, and I **know** My own and My own **know** Me, even as the Father **knows** Me and I **know** the Father; and I lay down My life for the sheep" (John 10:14–15).

The word "know" in this passage doesn't mean an academic understanding but knowledge through experience or relationship.

Jesus says the same way He intimately knows the Father is the same way we are to know Him. What an incredible reality! He doesn't merely know information about us, nor does He want us to know a bunch of facts about Him—He wants relationship.

This concept is further emphasized in God's name *Jehovah Raah*. Rô'eh, from which Raah is derived in Hebrew for the word "shepherd," can also be translated as "friend" or "companion"—Yahweh my friend.

The Lord is actively shepherding me, and because

He is my Good Shepherd, I do not lack anything as He supplies protection, provision, and direction. As His sheep, I experience His goodness and lovingkindness as I dwell in relationship with Him in the very place He is found.

GO DEEPER

1. Read Psalm 23 several times (preferably in various translations; see below). Much can be said about this wonderful psalm, but notice the transition in verse four from the language of "He" to "You" as David transitions from talking *about* God to talking directly *to* Him. What other insights about God being your Shepherd do you discover?

> **NASB** – *A Psalm of David. The LORD is my shepherd, I shall not want. He makes me lie down in green pastures; He leads me beside quiet waters. He restores my soul; He guides me in the paths of righteousness for His name's sake. Even though I walk through the valley of the shadow of death, I fear no evil, for You are with me; Your rod and Your staff, they comfort me. You prepare a table before me in the presence of my enemies; You have anointed my head with oil; my cup overflows. Surely goodness and lovingkindness will follow me all the days of my life, and I will dwell in the house of the LORD forever.*
>
> **LSB** – *A Psalm of David. Yahweh is my shepherd, I shall not want. He makes me lie down in green*

pastures; He leads me beside quiet waters. He restores my soul; He guides me in the paths of righteousness for His name's sake. Even though I walk through the valley of the shadow of death, I fear no evil, for You are with me; Your rod and Your staff, they comfort me. You prepare a table before me in the presence of my enemies; You have anointed my head with oil; my cup overflows. Surely goodness and lovingkindness will pursue me all the days of my life, and I will dwell in the house of Yahweh forever.

ESV - *A PSALM OF DAVID. The LORD is my shepherd; I shall not want. He makes me lie down in green pastures. He leads me beside still waters. He restores my soul. He leads me in paths of righteousness for his name's sake. Even though I walk through the valley of the shadow of death, I will fear no evil, for you are with me; your rod and your staff, they comfort me. You prepare a table before me in the presence of my enemies; you anoint my head with oil; my cup overflows. Surely goodness and mercy shall follow me all the days of my life, and I shall dwell in the house of the LORD forever.*

AMP - *A Psalm of David. THE LORD is my Shepherd [to feed, guide, and shield me], I shall not lack. He makes me lie down in [fresh, tender] green pastures; He leads me beside the still and restful waters. He refreshes and restores my life (my self); He leads me in the paths of righteousness [uprightness and right standing with Him—not for my earning it, but] for His name's sake. Yes, though I walk through the [deep, sunless] valley of the* shadow of death, I will fear or dread no evil, for You are with me; Your rod [to protect] and Your staff [to guide], they comfort me. You prepare a table before me in the presence of my enemies. You anoint my head with oil; my [brimming] cup runs over. Surely or only goodness, mercy, and unfailing love shall follow me all the days of my life, and through the length of my days the house of the Lord [and His presence] shall be my dwelling place.

CSB - *A psalm of David. The LORD is my shepherd; I have what I need. He lets me lie down in green pastures; he leads me beside quiet waters. He renews my life; he leads me along the right paths for his name's sake. Even when I go through the darkest valley, I fear no danger, for you are with me; your rod and your staff—they comfort me. You prepare a table before me in the presence of my enemies; you anoint my head with oil; my cup overflows. Only goodness and faithful love will pursue me all the days of my life, and I will dwell in the house of the LORD as long as I live.*

ISV - *A Davidic Psalm. The LORD is the one who is shepherding me; I lack nothing. He causes me to lie down in pastures of green grass; he guides me beside quiet waters. He revives my life; he leads me in pathways that are righteous for the sake of his name. Even when I walk through a valley of deep darkness, I will not be afraid because you are with me. Your rod and your staff—they comfort me. You prepare a table before me, even in the presence of my enemies. You anoint my head with oil; my cup* *overflows. Truly, goodness and gracious love will pursue me all the days of my life, and I will remain in the LORD's Temple forever.*

2. If you'd like to take these concepts deeper, here are three ideas (please note that links to the books, messages, and resources listed below can be found at deeperChristian.com/30day).
- I encourage you to read W. Philip Keller's shepherd trilogy, especially his classic book *A Shepherd Looks at the 23rd Psalm*.
- I've preached a couple of messages looking at the I AM statements of Jesus from John 10 and their relationship to Psalm 23. I'd encourage you to give them a listen.
- If you want to learn more about "hesed" and what God's mercy and lovingkindness means, I encourage you to read Michael Card's book *Inexpressible*. I also have several podcasts, articles, and resources on my website about hesed that you can dive into.

3. Ponder and reflect on Psalm 100:3. Spend time with your Good Shepherd and Lord, Jesus Christ. While praying for protection, provision, or direction is not wrong, remember that all you need is found in Him, and He will supply your every need.

Know that Yahweh, He is God; It is He who has made us, and not we ourselves; we are His people and the sheep of His pasture (Psalm 100:3).

DAY 18

EXTRAVAGANT FORGIVENESS

It is a fantastic realization that God doesn't merely forgive us; He forgives us *extravagantly*.

There is no deed He will not forgive, no lifestyle He cannot transform, no impurity He cannot purge.

His mercy, forgiveness, grace, and love are genuinely extravagant.

Each of us is guilty. "There is none righteous, not even one..." (Romans 3:10; Psalm 14:3). And as we've talked about before, even our best attempts at righteousness are but filthy rags (see Isaiah 64:6).

Yet, the wonder of the Gospel is that while we were living in selfishness, sin, and rebellion, Christ died for us (see Romans 5:8).

Jesus didn't pat us on the head and overlook the sin; He actually dealt with the penalty and the power of it on the cross. The death of Christ on the cross was the perfect sacrifice and atonement for our sins, so not only was the punishment removed (so you can experience life instead of death), but the cross also removed the power of sin (you no longer need to live under sin's tyrannical rule). You have been set free!

What has God done with our sin?
- "If we confess our sins, He is faithful and righteous to forgive us our sins and to cleanse us from all unrighteousness" (1 John 1:9).
- "As far as the east is from the west, so far has He removed our transgressions from us" (Psalm 103:12).
- "...but in love You have delivered my life from the pit of destruction, for You have cast all my sins behind Your back" (Isaiah 38:17b, ESV).
- "I, even I, am the one who wipes out your transgressions for My own sake, and I will not remember your sins" (Isaiah 43:25).
- "But You are a God of lavish forgiveness, gracious and compassionate, slow to anger and abounding in lovingkindness; and You did not forsake them" (Nehemiah 9:17b).
- "To the Lord our God belong compassion and forgiveness, for we have rebelled against Him..." (Daniel 9:9).
- "He will again have compassion on us; He will subdue our iniquities. And You will cast all their sins into the depths of the sea" (Micah 7:19). When Corrie ten Boom would speak on this verse, she would typically add that God also posted a "no fishing allowed" sign.[28]

Charles Spurgeon, talking about what God has done with our sin, declared:

This forgiveness, again, is given by the Lord Jesus Christ in the completest possible manner. He keeps no back reckonings; He retains no reserves of anger. He so forgives that He forgets. That is the wonder of it: He says, "I will not remember thy sins." He casts them behind His back; they are wholly and completely gone from His observation or regard. Alas, such is poor human nature, that even fathers, when they have forgiven a wayward child, will, perhaps, throw the offense in his teeth years after, when he again offends; but it is never so with Christ. He says, "Thy sins shall not be mentioned against thee any more forever." He has done with the sins of His people in so effectual a way that not a whisper concerning them shall ever come from His mouth so as to grieve them. They will themselves remember their sins with deep repentance; but the Lord will never challenge them on account of their past rebellions. Blessed be the name of Christ for such complete forgiveness as this.[29]

While this truth about forgiveness is likely not new to you, here is the point we often forget: we are to forgive others in the same manner that Christ has forgiven us.

Paul writes in Ephesians 4:32, "Be kind to one another, tender-hearted, graciously forgiving each other, **just as** God in Christ also has graciously forgiven you."

The little word "as," though two tiny letters, packs a punch. Just as Christ forgave me, so too I am to forgive others. How did Jesus forgive me? Extravagantly, without limit. He doesn't keep a tally of offenses (and I am beyond thankful He doesn't!).

Have you forgiven those who have hurt or offended you just as Jesus has forgiven you?

DAY 18

Today's Adventure:
Are you harboring resentment, bitterness, anger, frustration, or unforgiveness toward anyone? Is there anything from your past that needs to be dealt with? Are there any relationships that need restoration? Spend time before God and allow the Holy Spirit to reveal anything you need to deal with in your life. Are you willing for God to bring you to a place where you repent for your unforgiveness and practically forgive the people who hurt or offended you?

Tomorrow, we will discuss why forgiveness is so important and some ideas to get you started. I encourage you to be open and honest before the Lord today and list anything He brings to mind that you need to deal with others about. Whether you were the one who was hurt or you were the instigator and hurt others, both need to be dealt with in our lives.

GO DEEPER

True forgiveness is not something we produce in our own strength; instead, it is found in Christ (see 2 Corinthians 2:10b; Ephesians 1:7; Colossians 1:14). In Him, we have the forgiveness of our sins but also the strength and ability to forgive those who have sinned against us. Because of Him, we *can* forgive and love our enemies (see Matthew 5:44; Luke 6:27–28).

DAY 19

EXTRAVAGANT FORGIVENESS TOO

After talking about a shepherd going after a lost sheep, Jesus says, "Now if your brother sins, go and show him his fault, between you and him alone; if he listens to you, you have won your brother. But if he does not listen to you, take one or two more with you, so that by the mouth of two or three witnesses every fact may be confirmed. And if he refuses to listen to them, tell it to the church; and if he refuses to listen even to the church, let him be to you as the Gentile and the tax collector" (Matthew 18:15–17).

Though the passage is often used for church discipline, we must remember the passage's context is a shepherd going after a lost sheep. How should we treat a brother who sins against us? Go after him like a shepherd would seek out and restore a lost sheep—bang on his door, with hat in hand, knees buckled, shoulders stooped, and tears in your eyes, pleading with him to repent and turn from the sin.

And if he doesn't repent…gang up on him in love. Get a group all doing the same—with hat in hand and tears in eyes, pleading with him to return to God.

DAY 19

Peter then asks Jesus, "Lord, how often shall my brother sin against me and I forgive him? Up to seven times?" Jesus told him, "I do not say to you, up to seven times, but up to seventy times seven" (Matthew 18:21–22).

The question is a fair one. How many times do we need to keep doing this love thing and forgiving the one who hurts us?

In Peter's day, the Roman/Greek philosophy was "do unto others *before* they do unto you." The Jewish command was "do unto others *as* they do unto you." The Rabbis took it a step further and said to forgive three times before you return the hurt. So can you imagine the shock when Peter takes the count to another level and says "seven times"?!

Yet Jesus, in hyperbole, tells Peter to quit counting. Scholars are unsure if the correct translation of Jesus' words is 77 times or "70 times 7" (both can be correct in Greek)—in either case, it makes the same point: quit counting.

Jesus does not say to keep a record of wrongs, and when the person who offends you reaches 77 (or 490), you can stop forgiving them—the truth is, when we keep a record of wrongs, we are not practicing forgiveness.

After Peter's remark, Jesus tells the parable of a king settling accounts. The king called in a servant who owed him ten thousand talents—a talent equalling fifteen years worth of wages. This man owed the king 150,000 years worth of wages! Yet, the man told the king, "Have patience with me and I will repay you everything" (Matthew 18:26). Impossible! Yet, the king, moved with mercy and compassion, forgave the debt. Can you imagine what it would feel to have those chains of bondage removed?!

But what did the servant do? He found a fellow servant who owed him 100 days worth of wages and demanded the money, refused to show mercy, and threw the fellow servant in jail.

When the king heard, he called the servant back in and declared, "You wicked slave, I forgave you all that debt because you pleaded with me. Should you not also have had mercy on your fellow slave, in the same way that I had mercy on you?" (Matthew 18:32–33).

Jesus made the point: "My heavenly Father will also do the same to you, if each of you does not forgive his brother from your hearts" (Matthew 18:35).

How can we, in our arrogance, receive God's extravagant forgiveness without showing forgiveness to those who hurt us?

Stephen Manley once said, "No one will ever sin against you as much as you have sinned against God." And if God is willing to forgive us extravagantly, how can we be so prideful and arrogant not to forgive those who offend us?

Remember yesterday's message: "Instead, be kind to one another, tender-hearted, graciously forgiving each other, just as God in Christ also has graciously forgiven you" (Ephesians 4:32). Paul said the same thing in Colossians 3:12–14,

> "Put on then, as God's chosen ones, holy and beloved, compassionate hearts, kindness, humility, meekness, and patience, bearing with one another and, if one has a complaint against another, **forgiving each other; as the Lord has forgiven you, so you also must forgive**. And above all these put on love, which binds everything together in perfect harmony" (ESV).

Forgiveness is a demonstration of love. And you are to be known by your love for one another (see John 13:34–35).

Today's Adventure:
Seek reconciliation with those around you.

Jesus has reconciled us to Himself, and we are now to have a ministry of reconciliation (see 2 Corinthians 5:17–21).

If there is unforgiveness, bitterness, hatred, strife, anger, etc., go make it right with that person. We are told not to wait for the offender to apologize but to initiate and forgive them (see Matthew 5:22–24; Mark 11:25–26). And if you were the one who caused the sin, pain, or offense, then you need to go, apologize, and make it right.

You are not responsible for the other person's response, but you are responsible for your obedience.

I realize not every situation is simple, and there are times when the person who caused you pain may no longer be alive or where it may be prudent not to address the individual who hurt you directly (e.g., in the case of abuse). In such scenarios, seek the wisdom and godly counsel from a pastor or trusted mentor who can walk with you through a process of forgiveness, healing, and reconciliation. Regardless, we are still called to forgive even in those difficult situations.

Forgive, even as Christ Jesus extravagantly forgave you.

And be thankful He keeps no record of wrongs.

GO DEEPER

My friend Eric Ludy explains the difference between "human-born forgiveness" (what we can do in our own strength) and "spirit-born forgiveness" (that which we are called to as Christians, and only God can do in and through us):

- ***Human-born forgiveness*** *has made the choice to no longer hold the offense against the person, and it has chosen to stew about the grievance no more. It brings about a bland, non-feeling blankness of soul towards the offending person. It no longer hates, but it also doesn't love. This sort of forgiveness saves us from the deadly effects of resentment and bitterness, but finds nothing of the robust power of Christ in the forgiveness process. For after all is said and done, the fault is still remembered even though it is no longer resented.*
- ***Spirit-born forgiveness*** *not only frees the captive from the net of resentment, but it frees their fault from the net of one's remembrance. It is fault forgotten, removed from the equation of relationship. And Christianity doesn't offer neutrality, a bland, non-feeling blank soul response to the now forgiven soul, but rather, it offers kindness, warmth of being, tenderhearted forgiveness—it offers love. The forgiven, now becomes the object of love and specific prayer—with an honest God-deposited desire to see them triumph in Christ Jesus.*[30]

If you want to go deeper with this concept of forgiveness

and reconciliation, I encourage you to listen to Eric Ludy's messages: *Power to Forgive* and *Power to Reconcile*. You can find links to both of these sermons at deeperChristian.com/30day.

DAY 20

JEHOVAH MEKODDISHKEM

Yahweh who Sanctifies

Leonard Ravenhill rightly said, "You know, we live in a day when we are more afraid of holiness than we are of sinfulness."

Though holiness has received a bad rap in the church today, holiness is not legalistic or a list of dos and don'ts; holiness is the nature of our God.

When Isaiah saw the Lord high and lifted up (Isaiah 6), the seraphim were not crying out that God was holy. They didn't even say He was holy holy. Do you know how holy our God is? The only way to describe the holiness of our God is to use a triple emphasis—"Holy, Holy, Holy, is Yahweh of hosts; the whole earth is full of His glory" (6:3).

HOLINESS

The idea of holiness is to be set apart, separate, or other than.

DAY 20

When the Israelites were preparing to enter the Promise Land, God told them they were going into a place where they were not to be like the nations around them; they were called to be separate, other than, set apart, holy. They were not to look or act like the world around them, for God had called them to be like Himself—"You shall be holy, for I, Yahweh your God, am holy.... Thus you shall be holy to Me, for I Yahweh am holy; and I have separated you from the peoples to be Mine" (Leviticus 19:2; 20:26).

Strangely, the church in our modern-day has turned holiness into something negative, an "oh bummer, I can't do this or that." But biblically, holiness is never mentioned in the negative; it is always positive. It is less about what you DON'T get to do and more about what you DO get to do! Sure, you don't get to live like the world in their twisted thinking and living, but you do get to have a relationship with the King of the Universe and have His life indwelling and sourcing your life! This is not a "bummer, I don't get to do my favorite sin," but rather, "Praise Jesus, I don't have to live under the tyranny of sin but can walk in victory!"

I love what one author said,

> *"In the early church, Christians never had any doubt that they must be different from the world; they, in fact, knew that they must be so different that the probability was that the world would kill them and certainly was that the world would hate them. But the tendency in the modern church has been to play down the difference between the church and the world. We have, in effect, often said to people: 'As*

long as you live a decent, respectable life, it is quite all right to become a church member and to call yourself a Christian. You don't need to be so very different from other people.' [When] in fact, Christians should be easily identifiable in the world."[31]

Christ does not take us out of the world, but He does make us different within the world.

FILTHY RAGS

God, who is holy, calls us to be holy because He is holy (see Exodus 19:6; Leviticus 19:2; 20:7; 20:26; 21:8; 1 Thessalonians 4:7; 1 Peter 1:16).

Yet our problem is that we cannot be holy in and of ourselves. The best we can pull off is "filthy rags" (see Isaiah 64:6). Awkwardly, the word Isaiah uses for "filthy rags" is talking about a woman's menstrual cloth—or putting it into today's language—all our righteousness is like a dirty used tampon.

In other words, we are *not* holy.

If our best attempts at holiness and righteousness are filthy rags, how can we be holy?

BECOMING HOLY

God has "intrinsic holiness"—meaning He is the only one whose nature is holy in and of Himself. If anything else is holy, it is derived from Him; in other words, when the Holy God comes upon something or someone, it also becomes holy.

For example, Moses likely had been to Mount Sinai

countless times during his 40 years as a shepherd. He may have been there the day before, allowing his sheep to wander its slopes and eat the grass and shrubs. But on one particular day, as a bush began to burn without burning up, God spoke from the bush, saying, "Remove your sandals from your feet, for the place on which you are standing is holy ground" (Exodus 3:5).

What made the ground holy? Moments before, Moses was fine wearing sandals and walking the slopes; now, he must treat the place as holy. Why?

Because God showed up.

The secret to holiness is not attempting to be holy in and of yourself (remember the "filthy rags"?); instead, the secret to holiness is embracing the one who is holy.

1 Thessalonians 5:23-24 says, "Now may the God of peace Himself **sanctify you entirely**, and may your spirit and soul and body be preserved complete, without blame at the coming of our Lord Jesus Christ. Faithful is He who calls you, who also will do it." Notice Paul's progression: sanctification (the process of being made holy) begins within (spirit and soul) and works its way out to your body and actions.

Jesus told the scribes and Pharisees that if you want the outside to be clean, start on the inside (see Matthew 23:25-26).

We can't merely focus on outward actions and think we've become holy. Holiness is more about the insides—the heart, the motives, the attitude—than the actions themselves. Yes, the actions are important, but if you merely deal with the action and not the heart, it is still unholy.

Too often, as Christians, we want God to deal with

our actions or bad habits rather than allow Him to change our hearts and minds. We want Him to remove the problems people see but not change the source of those actions. Yet, if God transforms our hearts and minds, the actions will eventually follow.

"Therefore I exhort you, brothers, by the mercies of God, to present your bodies as a sacrifice—living, holy, and pleasing to God, which is your spiritual service of worship. And do not be conformed to this world, but be transformed by the renewing of your mind, so that you may approve what the will of God is, that which is good and pleasing and perfect" (Romans 12:1–2).

THE LORD WHO SANCTIFIES

Here's some good news: while the best we can produce in ourselves is filthy rags, God, the Holy One, wants to transform us and set us apart for His use, purpose, and delight.

Peter tells us, "As obedient children, not being conformed to the former lusts which were yours in your ignorance, but like the Holy One who called you, be holy yourselves also in all your conduct; because it is written, "YOU SHALL BE HOLY, FOR I AM HOLY" (1 Peter 1:14–16).

Yet God doesn't merely call us to an impossible standard in hopes that we "try our best"; instead, He is the one who sanctifies us.

In calling the Israelites to live set apart and holy, God tells them, "Therefore, you shall set yourselves apart as holy and be holy, for I am Yahweh your God. And you shall keep My statutes and do them; I am Yahweh who makes you holy" (Leviticus 20:7–8). In this passage, God gives another of His majestic names—Jehovah Mekoddishkem, "Yahweh who makes you holy," or "The LORD who sanctifies you."

Mekoddishkem, or *M'kaddesh*, comes from the Hebrew word (qadash/kaddesh), which means "to sanctify" or "make holy." While *kaddesh* appears hundreds of times in the Bible, the name only appears twice (Leviticus 20:8 and Exodus 31:13)—and the emphasis is on the fact that He is the one who brings about the sanctification. Yes, we must humble ourselves and consecrate ourselves before the Lord, but He does the inner work of healing, cleansing, and transformation.

We may not be able to produce holiness in ourselves, but we *can* live holy lives as we embrace the Holy One who longs to sanctify us. Jesus…Jehovah Mekoddishkem…is His name.

Remember, you are called to be separate and other than the world around you. Yes, you may be in the world, but the world is not to be in you.

GO DEEPER

1. Read the following passages and consider them in light of God's holiness and His command for you to be holy: Exodus 15:11; Leviticus 11:44–45; 1 Samuel 2:2; Psalm 5:4; 29:2; Isaiah 57:15; John 17:17; Hebrews 10:10; 1 Peter 3:15–16; 2 Peter 3:13; 1 John 1:5–9; 2:15–17; Revelation 4:8; 15:4; 21:27.

2. Spend time with God and allow the Holy Spirit to search your life for any sin, impurity, selfishness, or

pride (see Psalm 139:23-24). Don't rush; be humble, surrender yourself, and give God the right to open any door and peek into every crevice of your heart and mind. Consider writing down a list of anything He brings to mind. Call sin for what it really is: sin. Confess and repent before the Lord, trusting that "If we confess our sins, He is faithful and righteous to forgive us our sins and to cleanse us from all unrighteousness" (1 John 1:9). And if you need to make something right with someone, don't put it off, but go to them and ask for forgiveness. If you need help getting started, consider walking prayerfully through the 21 questions from the Holy Club of Oxford (which can be found at deeperChristian.com/30day).

Search me, O God, and know my heart; try me and know my anxious thoughts; and see if there be any hurtful way in me, and lead me in the everlasting way (Psalm 139:23-24).

DAY 21

ALL IN ON JESUS

There is a good indication that Jesus quoted the Shema every day of his life.

The Shema, literally meaning "hear" or "listen," is the first word in Deuteronomy 6:4–5: "Hear *[shema]*, O Israel! Yahweh is our God, Yahweh is one! You shall love Yahweh your God with all your heart and with all your soul and with all your might."

This passage was the basic confession of faith in Judaism and central in the life of an Israelite from the time of Moses to today. In Jesus' day, every Jew would quote the Shema at the beginning of the day and often at its end. This was the passage that the men quoted every week at the start of the service in the synagogue. It was foundational to the life of Israel, and as such, many scholars suggest Jesus likely quoted it daily.

Since many rabbis saw the Shema as the heart of the entire Law (in fact, some modern scholars suggest that the whole book of Deuteronomy is a commentary or explanation of the Shema), it is no wonder Jesus used this as His response when asked what the greatest commandment was:

Jesus answered, "The most important is, 'Hear, O Israel: The Lord our God, the Lord is one. And you shall love the Lord your God with all your heart and with all your soul and with all your mind and with all your strength' [Deuteronomy 6:4–5]. The second is this: 'You shall love your neighbor as yourself' [Leviticus 19:18]. There is no other commandment greater than these" (Mark 12:29–31, ESV).

LOVING GOD WITH EVERYTHING

In ancient Hebrew, "heart" (which included the mind) and "soul" overlapped, so rather than being two distinct aspects of a person, they conveyed the idea of the "internal life, dispositions, emotions, and intellect"[32] (one scholar said we might better understand it today as the whole of our mind and emotions, both conscious and unconscious). "Strength" (or "might") indicates strength or power, but also energy and ability. Taking the passage as a whole, the emphasis is upon loving God with totality, undivided loyalty, wholehearted and exclusive devotion.

I find it fascinating that Jesus, like He often did when He explained the Old Testament, gave a fuller understanding of the passage. The original in Deuteronomy says, "You shall love Yahweh your God with all your **heart** and with all your **soul** and with all your **might**."

Yet, when Jesus quoted the passage, He added "mind." Though covered in the Shema with "heart," for a Greek-influenced world that emphasized the mind, it appears

Jesus didn't want His audience to have any excuses; their love and devotion unto God was to be total and all-consuming.

If we quickly look at each aspect of loving God with "all," we find there is nothing excluded:

- **Heart**: heart, interior, center; the locus of a person's thoughts (mind), volition, emotions, and knowledge of right from wrong (conscience) understood as the heart
- **Soul**: the immaterial part of a person which is the active or motivating source of their life; the site of all the psychological facilities (such as the heart, mind, and conscience)
- **Mind**: understanding, intelligence, mind, disposition, thought; that which is responsible for one's thoughts and feelings, especially the seat of the faculty of reason
- **Might**: capability, strength, power, might; the possession of qualities required to do something or get something done

As the Bible Knowledge Commentary puts it: "To love the Lord means to choose Him for an intimate relationship and to obey His commands. This command, to love Him, is given often in Deuteronomy (6:5; 7:9; 10:12; 11:1, 13, 22; 13:3; 19:9; 30:6, 16, 20). Loving Him was to be wholehearted (with all your heart) and was to pervade every aspect of an Israelite's being and life (soul and strength)."[33]

Today's Adventure:
List how you can practically love God with ALL your heart, soul, mind, and strength.

DAY 21

How can you begin to take action today and this week?

Loving Jesus isn't to be a theory we mull around in our minds; instead, it is demonstrated in how we live—it is revealed in action. Does your life genuinely show that you love Him with ALL?

Jesus told us the summary of the Law is to love God. Tomorrow, we will analyze the second aspect: loving others.

GO DEEPER

Consider examining these passages in light of loving Jesus with wholehearted and exclusive devotion:

- Deuteronomy 10:12–13
- 2 Chronicles 6:14
- Psalm 84:1–2, 10; 119:2
- Jeremiah 29:13–14
- Matthew 6:33
- John 14:15–27; 15:1–13
- 1 Corinthians 13
- Colossians 1:18
- Hebrews 11:6
- 1 John 1:5–7; 2:15–17; 3:10, 16–18; 4:7–21

DAY 22

LOVING OUR NEIGHBORS

"You shall love the Lord your God with all your heart, and with all your soul, and with all your strength, and with all your mind; and your neighbor as yourself" (Luke 10:27).

Yesterday, we briefly examined the first part of the great commandment—loving God with wholehearted and exclusive devotion. All in. Nothing held back.

Several scholars have pointed out that Jesus' statement, "And the second is like it: 'You shall love your neighbor as yourself'" (Matthew 22:39), does not indicate an order of importance; instead, the two statements are equally significant. In other words, Jesus does not tell us to love God and, if we have extra energy, to love our neighbor. He declares that both are essential to the Christian life.

If you do not love others, then you do not love God, and if you love God with wholehearted and exclusive devotion, love for others will naturally come out of you (see 1 John 3:10–11, 16–18; 4:7–8, 11–12, 16; also John 13:35; 15:17; 17:17–26).

Our love for others should indeed be a byproduct of our love for God—that as we love Him, He fills us with His love and enables us to love those around us—but biblically, the two commands carry equal weights.

As I love others, I demonstrate love to God (see Matthew 25:40); when I love God, I won't be able to withhold love from others. They are intricately tied together.

In Luke's account, the lawyer who questioned Jesus wanted to justify himself and asked, "And who is my neighbor?" (Luke 10:29).

Interestingly, this was a question the rabbis often debated. They wanted to fulfill the command in Leviticus 19:18, but with the Roman occupation, Greek philosophy running rampant, and a host of other "exclusions" they tried to justify, many rabbis declared that "neighbor" only referred to fellow Israelites, who were not Roman informers or religious heretics. And even some Pharisees only included fellow Pharisees as "neighbors" to the exclusion of everyone else.

So, who is our neighbor?

Jesus previously declared, "You have heard that it was said, 'You shall love your neighbor and hate your enemy.' But I say to you, love your enemies and pray for those who persecute you…" (Matthew 5:43–44).

To answer the lawyer's question, Jesus tells a story that reveals more than just whom we are obligated to love.

A man was going down from Jerusalem to Jericho, and fell among robbers, and they stripped him and beat him, and went away leaving him half dead (Luke 10:30).

This seventeen-mile journey was not only difficult but extremely dangerous. The steep, narrow road descends 3600 feet from Jerusalem's hills to the lowest city on earth, Jericho, 846 feet below sea level. Due to its remote location, it was often a place where robbers waited for travelers to pass by, and as such, it was foolish to travel there alone. No one would have been surprised when the man was robbed and left half dead.

And a priest happened to be going down on that road, and when he saw him, he passed by on the other side. Likewise a Levite also, when he came to the place and saw him, passed by on the other side (Luke 10:31–32).

Since the priest and Levite (a clerical aid at the temple) were coming *down* the road, it is presumed they finished their duties at the temple and have now returned to Jericho, a city where many important temple priests and workers lived. Men of such importance would not have walked the seventeen-mile journey; they were likely riding a donkey and had a small group with them for protection. They had everything they needed to help the half-dead man on the path.

It is important to note that because the man was stripped and lying naked on the road, there was no way to identify him—neither his social status nor nationality, which were typically determined by speech or clothing.

Yet, both the priest and the Levite saw the man lying in the road and decided to refuse compassion despite being men who were known for living to the letter of the law. Because the priest and Levite would have been of high social status in Israel and thus admired by the crowds, their response was likely understood and justified by those who listened to Jesus' parable.

When most of us think of the priest and Levite passing by on the "other side," we think of a large road where they can stay far away and act as if they didn't see the man lying there. Yet the road from Jerusalem to Jericho is narrow, often no more than a few feet across. There was no way they could have missed seeing the man and likely had to step over him to pass by.

In typical Jewish storytelling, the crowd likely expected to hear that the third character, the hero, was a good Jewish man. Jesus has been descending the order of importance from priest to Levite, so it would have been natural to assume the next character was a good and honorable Jew.

Yet, Jesus turns the tables by choosing a Samaritan.

Jews despised Samaritans. They were the half-Jew, half-Gentile people who lived in the middle of Israel and were so hated that Jews would walk an extra three days to go around their land if they needed to go from Galilee in the north to Jerusalem in the south.

> *But a Samaritan, who was on a journey, came upon him, and when he saw him, he felt compassion. And he came to him and bandaged up his wounds, pouring oil and wine on them, and he put him on his own animal, and brought him to an inn and took care of him. And on the next day he took out two denarii and gave them to the innkeeper and said, "Take care of him, and whatever more you spend, when I return I will repay you" (Luke 10:33–35).*

This Samaritan saw the man lying on the road and used oil and wine as a medicinal treatment, likely using his own clothing (his keffiyeh headscarf or linen undergarment) to wrap the wounds. Placing the hurt man on his donkey, the Samaritan walked the rest of the way to an inn and used his own money to pay not just for one night, but scholars tell us that the two denarii paid to the innkeeper would have been enough for twenty-four days, promising to come back and give even more if it was needed.

The lawyer who asked Jesus the original question, "Who is my neighbor?" wanted to know whom he was obligated to help and who his neighbor was. But Jesus turns the question upside down. Rather than clarifying who qualifies as a neighbor and who does not, Jesus asks, "Which of these three do you think **proved** to be a neighbor to the man who fell into the robbers' hands?" (Luke 10:36).

The lawyer responds (notice he was unwilling to use the word "Samaritan"), "The one who showed mercy toward him" (Luke 10:37).

The question Jesus asked the lawyer was not "Who is the neighbor you need to help?"—splitting the world into groups of people we are supposed to love or not—the question was "Who proved to be a neighbor?" Who acted with love and mercy?

Jesus tore down the dividing wall of hostility and doesn't split people into groups we are called to love and those we can justifiably hate (see Ephesians 2:11–22). If God is love, and He loved us even while we were yet sinners living in rebellion against Him (see Romans 5:8), then there is not a single person we can withhold love and mercy from.

Then Jesus said to him, "Go and do the same" (Luke 10:37).

Today's Adventure:
What can you practically do today to show love and mercy to those around you?

and

Is there anyone you are angry or frustrated with? Is there someone you hate and can't forgive? Is there a people group you look down upon because of their choices, behavior, nationality, or _____? Would you be willing for God to showcase His love and mercy in and through your life to that person(s)? Are you willing to love your neighbor as much or more than you love yourself?

Let's admit that we *really* do love ourselves—we protect and pamper ourselves, feed ourselves food we enjoy, and most of our day is filled with thoughts about ourselves. What if we had the same intensity of love and obsession for those around us?

While we don't have to agree with someone's behavior or overlook their sin, we are called to demonstrate God's love and mercy to the world. We are asked to give of ourselves—our time, money, energy, resources—on behalf of others.

We don't have to agree with the choices someone

makes, the behavior they indulge in, or the sin they commit—but we need God's heart and love for that person.

Do we have that kind of love for others? Do we have the kind of love that is willing to go to a cross and bleed, suffer, and die for the sake of those around us?

If I love Jesus, I will love others. And as I love others, my love for Jesus will deepen.

"You shall love the Lord your God with **all** your **heart**, and with **all** your **soul**, and with **all** your **strength**, and with **all** your **mind**, and... **you shall love your neighbor as yourself**. On these two commandments hang the whole Law and the Prophets" (Luke 10:27 and Matthew 22:39–40).

GO DEEPER

We often misunderstand the parable of the Good Samaritan because we hyper-analyze every detail rather than see the story for what it is. Below, I've included a modern "Good Samaritan" story by Gary M. Burge, which may help deepen your understanding of what it means to "love your neighbor."

> *By making every element bear some meaning, we will introduce ideas into the parables that are completely foreign to them. In the last century scholars emphasized that at the heart of each parables lies a crisis—a point or points of stark contrast that shock us, forcing us to make a value judgment on a theme or character....*
>
> *One of the parables most commonly subject*

to abuse is the parable of the good Samaritan. Christians have regularly sought meaning in each element of the story. The wounded man means one thing, the donkey of the Samaritan another, the inn that gives him aid still another. I was discussing this problem with a Middle Eastern Christian once and he told me that we in the West have utterly lost the meaning of the story. So, in Jerusalem one afternoon he told me his own [true] version of it:

Not long ago in Jerusalem's famed Hadasseh Hospital, an Israeli soldier lay dying. He had contracted AIDS as a result of his gay lifestyle and was not in the last stages of the disease's terrible course. His father was a famous Jerusalem rabbi, and both he and the rest of his family had disowned him. He was condemned to die in his shame. The nursing staff on his floor knew his story and carefully avoided his room. Everyone was simply waiting for his life to expire.

The soldier happened to be a part of a regiment that patrolled the Occupied West Bank, and his unit was known for its ferocity and war-fighting skills. The Palestinians living in occupation hated these troops. They were merciless and could be cruel. Their green berets always gave them away.

One evening the soldier went into cardiac arrest. All the usual alarms went off, but the nursing staff did not respond. Even the doctors looked the other way. Yet on the floor another man was at work — a Palestinian Christian janitor — who knew this story as well as also knew the meaning of the emergency. Incredibly, he was a man whose village *had been attacked by this soldier's unit. When the Palestinian heard the alarm and witnessed the neglect, his heart was filled with compassion. He dropped his broom, entered the soldier's room, and attempted to resuscitate the man by giving him cardiopulmonary resuscitation [CPR]. The scene was remarkable: a poor Palestinian man, a victim of this soldier's violence, now tried to save his enemy while those who should have been doing this stood on the sidelines.*

My Arab Christian friend told me: when you understand this story, you will understand the parable of the good Samaritan. When you understand what it means for an enemy to love an enemy — and for the righteous to show neglect — then you will have a picture of the power of God's grace at work in a person's heart.[34]

DAY 23

STUDY FOR YOURSELF

*Jehovah Nissi or Jehovah Tsidkenu
or El Elyon*

Today, I want to do something a bit different. I want you to choose one of the names of God below and study it yourself. While I'd encourage you to study all of them eventually, pick at least one to focus on today.

As you do, don't let it become a mere academic study but rather be still and spend time with God Himself (see Psalm 46:10). This is an adventure to know Him more. Use the passages provided as a springboard for your study of that name.

FOR EACH NAME, ANSWER THE FOLLOWING QUESTIONS:

- **What does this name tell you about the character, nature, attributes, and life of God?**
- **How does Jesus fulfill (or embody/exhibit) the meaning of this name?** *(consider expanding your study of this concept into the New Testament)*
- **How does your life practically change by knowing God through this name?**

DAY 23

JEHOVAH TSIDKENU (THE LORD OUR RIGHTEOUSNESS)

- Jehovah Tsidkenu occurs only two times in the Old Testament, in Jeremiah 23:6 and 33:16.
- Tsedek, from which Tsidkenu is derived, means "to be stiff," "to be straight," or "righteous" in Hebrew.
- Note the progression of this name. In Jeremiah 23:6, the name of the coming Messiah is called "The Lord our Righteousness," but in 33:16, the city where God's presence dwells (Jerusalem) takes on the name, and thus the righteousness, of God. So, too, as Christians, we are to bear the name (and thus the nature) of Christ in our lives as His Spirit dwells within us.
- Passages to help you start your study: Jeremiah 23:6 and 33:16.
- See also: Genesis 15:6; Isaiah 61:10; 64:6; Ezekiel 36:26–27; 1 Corinthians 1:30; 2 Corinthians 5:17–21; Philippians 1:11; 3:9; 2 Peter 1:1

JEHOVAH NISSI (THE LORD OUR BANNER)

- Jehovah Nissi occurs only one time in Exodus 17:15.
- Nissi comes from the word meaning "banner, ensign, standard, or flag" and was the banner or flag (usually with an insignia or picture on it) brought to the frontlines of a battle under which an army fought, found hope, and kept their focus.

- Throughout history, a banner often served three purposes:
  1. to identify a group (i.e., each of the twelve tribes of Israel had a standard, see Numbers 2:2)
  2. to claim possession of space or territory (to plant a flag/banner would declare victory; would be used to direct a path or route to a city, like a road sign; or used to mark a boundary to a country)
  3. to lend festivity to a celebration (see Song of Songs 2:4)
- Passages to help you start your study:
  Exodus 17:1-16; Numbers 21:8-9; Psalm 20:5; 60:4; Isaiah 11:10-12; Zechariah 9:16

EL ELYON
(THE MOST HIGH GOD)

- El Elyon occurs 28 times in the Old Testament, 19 of which are in the Psalms. "Elyon" literally means "most high," and when combined with "El" (God), the translation would be "God Most High." This name expresses the extreme sovereignty, majesty, and preeminence of God. It reminds us that He alone is supreme, the most powerful, and is over all others; therefore, we can place our trust and hope in Him.
- Passages to help you start your study:
  Genesis 14:18-22; Psalm 7:17; 57:1-3; 78:35; 91:9; Daniel 4:34; 7:22; Acts 16:17
- See also: Psalm 37:1-7; Proverbs 3:5-6; 29:25;

DAY 23

Lamentations 3:24; Ephesians 1:19–23;
Philippians 2:9–11; Colossians 1:15–20; 2:9–10;
2 Thessalonians 2:16

DAY 24

UNDISTRACTED DEVOTION

Distracted
dis·tract | də'strak(t)
adjective
unable to concentrate because one's mind is preoccupied

Martha was doing what her culture told her to do—be hospitable, make a meal for her guests, and stay in the women's area. Her sister Mary was doing the opposite by sitting at the feet of Jesus in the common room where (typically) only the men were allowed.

But Martha was distracted with all her preparations; and she came up to Him and said, "Lord, do You not care that my sister has left me to do all the preparations alone? Then tell her to help me." But the Lord answered and said to her, "Martha, Martha, you are worried and bothered about so many things, but only one thing is necessary, for Mary has chosen the good part, which shall not be taken away from her" (Luke 10:40–42).

DAY 24

Jesus defended and praised Mary for doing what was culturally unthinkable. Martha got a rebuke. One was devoted, the other distracted.

Distraction isn't about whether something is good or bad; it is *anything* that prevents you from giving your full attention to what you should focus on.

We, as a culture, live distracted. When we are at work, we think about our families or the vacation we want to take. When we are with our families, we are distracted by work. We sit down for a meal with someone and pull out our phones. We keep the beeps and buzzes on at all times of the day, pulled from whatever we are doing to check the latest email, social media post, text message, or cat video on YouTube.

Our lives are a blur of noise and distraction.

No wonder we are told to "cease striving and know that I am God" (Psalm 46:10)—or as the NKJV translates it, "Be still, and know I am God"—and that was commanded even before TV, internet, or cellphones.

There is a distinct correlation between slowing down to know God and being still enough to do so. You can't rush getting to know someone, not sincerely. Intimacy and relationships take time.

Martha wasn't doing something evil; it was good, but she was distracted. She should have thrown off every distraction (no matter how good and right) and placed her entire focus and devotion upon Jesus—like Mary.

We often equate our busyness with our significance. Because we rush around and our schedules are packed, our lives must be full and meaningful. Right? Yet, as Corrie ten Boom often warned in her messages, "Beware the barrenness of a busy life."

If you desire to know Jesus and grow in your relationship with Him, you must take time, without distraction, to pursue Him.

A.W. Tozer rightly said, "It is well that we accept the hard truth now: the man who would know God must give time to Him! He must count no time wasted, which is spent in the cultivation of His acquaintance."[35] Jim Elliot reminds us, "Wherever you are, be all there! Live to the hilt every situation you believe to be the will of God."[36]

Do you have distractions in your life? I challenge you to take a season and live with undistracted devotion.

Today's Adventure:
What distracts you? Would you commit to taking the next several days (through the end of the 30-day adventure) and remove anything that distracts you so you can intentionally go after Christ?

If it's media and entertainment—then take a media fast from all sources like TV, internet, and movies. If social media is your thing, let it go for a week. If you're distracted by the news, stop listening to it. If it's all the beeps and buzzes from your devices, turn off notifications and commit only to check it once or twice a day (this was incredibly freeing in my life). Maybe it's certain foods that make you tired and mentally foggy.

You likely already know what distracts you; if not, begin to pay attention to what turns your focus away from Jesus throughout the day.

Remove the distractions and then use these next few

days to intentionally pursue Jesus Christ through His Word, prayer, worship, etc.

Don't worry; all the distractions will still be there if you decide to return to something at the end of the adventure...but perhaps you won't want to return to the diversions as you discover greater freedom, joy, and intimacy with Christ.

Be still. And know

> *You will make known to me the **path of life**;*
> *in Your presence is **fullness of joy**;*
> *in Your right hand there are **pleasures forever**.*
> *Psalm 16:11*

GO DEEPER

If you need something to fill the extra time on your hands:

- Read through the entire New Testament
- Choose a book of the Bible and read it through as many times as you can in the next five days
- Spend an extended time in prayer
- Worship
- Make a list of the attributes, character, nature, and promises of God
- Memorize a longer passage like 1 Corinthians 13 or Romans 8:31–39
- Write notes of encouragement or prayers and send them to people God lays on your heart
- Pick a passage or topic and do an in-depth study on it

- Go for a long walk and use the time to ponder and commune with Jesus
- Be still and listen

DAY 25

OBSESSION

Oswald Chambers once asked, "Are you obsessed by something? You will probably say, 'No, by nothing,' but all of us are obsessed by something—usually by ourselves, or, if we are Christians, by our own experience of the Christian life. But the psalmist says that we are to be obsessed by God. The abiding awareness of the Christian life is to be God Himself, not just thoughts about Him. The total being of our life inside and out is to be absolutely obsessed by the presence of God."[37]

All of us are obsessed with something.

Looking at the world today, it doesn't take long to discover that entertainment, sports, sex, success, and the like have become the central passion and focus for most people.

The problem is not obsession itself; we were made to be obsessed. The question is: what will we be obsessed with?

Generally, three things reveal our obsession(s):

1. **Your Calendar** (time) – where do you spend your free time?
2. **Your Checkbook** (money) – what do you spend your money on?

3. **Your Conversation** (speech) – what do you talk about?

Typically, how we spend our time, what we spend money on, and what we talk about reveals what is most important to us.

If we looked at those three areas of your life, would it reveal that you are obsessed with Jesus?

THE SPORTS FANATIC

Could you imagine a guy standing up and declaring, "I'm a sports fanatic!" So you ask him what his favorite sport is. "I don't have one," is his reply. So you ask him what his favorite team is. "I don't have one of those either." We change tactics and ask if he will watch the Super Bowl or the NBA Finals this year. "Probably not," he responds.

Wouldn't you look at the guy and question if he really is a sports fanatic?

Similarly, could you imagine someone standing up and declaring, "I'm a Christian!" So, you ask them if they read the Bible. "Well, I bring it to church on Sundays." "Oh, so you go to church?" we ask. "Well, sometimes, mainly on the days I know there will be a potluck." We ask them about their prayer life. "Well, I pray before some meals."

I don't mean to judge, but wouldn't you look at the individual and question whether they are a Christian?

Christianity is not determined by what we DO; what we do should naturally flow from our relationship with Jesus.

If we are obsessed with Jesus, we can't help but spend

time in His Word because we want to know Him more. If we are obsessed with Him, we will delight in prayer so we can commune and converse with Him throughout the day. The more we obsess over Jesus, the more we should desire to spend time with His body, the church (potlucks are only a bonus).

Praying, reading the Bible, or attending church *doesn't* make you a Christian. But if you are a Christian with an obsession with Jesus, we couldn't stop you from prayer, reading, fellowship, evangelism, etc. Those would naturally flow out of your life. You couldn't help yourself!

So, what are you obsessed with?

Oswald Chambers finished his statement about obsession by saying, "If we are obsessed by God, nothing else can get into our lives—not concerns, nor tribulation, nor worries. And now we understand why our Lord so emphasized the sin of worrying. How can we dare to be so absolutely unbelieving when God totally surrounds us? To be obsessed by God is to have an effective barricade against all the assaults of the enemy."[38]

Don't you want to be more obsessed with Jesus?

Today's Adventure:
What are three things you can begin to do today to cultivate a greater obsession for Jesus in your life?

GO DEEPER

Consider the chorus of the hymn, *Turn Your Eyes Upon Jesus*,[39] in light of obsession:

DAY 25

Turn your eyes upon Jesus
Look full in His wonderful face
And the things of earth will grow strangely dim
In the light of His glory and grace

DAY 26

QANNĀ

Jealous

Jealousy is a...good thing?

The question lingered in my mind as I pondered God's obscure name...*Qannā*, Jealous.

I don't know about you, but I've always viewed jealousy as a negative thing, something we shouldn't have in our lives, and certainly something God wouldn't have. Sure, I've heard the passages where God says He is a jealous God, but because we often associate jealousy with envy or anger, I've had difficulty applying this attribute to God.

Even the three most popular books on God's attributes and character leave out His jealousy, and most dictionary definitions paint jealousy negatively. As such, we either misunderstand it or don't know what to do with it. Because we often see jealousy as a result of personal or relational insecurity, we presume that if God is jealous, it must mean He is an abusive or insecure God (as most Christian books portray His jealousy, if they even mention it).

Yet, over the past year, God's jealousy has become

one of the most beautiful aspects of His nature to me. As Christians, we must ask ourselves, where would we be if God was not jealous?

A JEALOUS GOD

God tells us six times[40] in Scripture He is jealous and that His name is Jealous (Qannā)...

- You shall not worship them or serve them; **for I, Yahweh your God, am a jealous God**, visiting the iniquity of the fathers on the children, on the third and the fourth generations of those who hate Me... (Exodus 20:5).
- ...for you shall not worship any other god, **for Yahweh, whose name is Jealous, is a jealous God**... (Exodus 34:14).
- For Yahweh your God is a consuming fire, **a jealous God** (Deuteronomy 4:24).
- You shall not worship them or serve them; **for I, Yahweh your God, am a jealous God**, visiting the iniquity of the fathers on the children and on the third and the fourth generations of those who hate Me... (Deuteronomy 5:9).
- ...**for Yahweh your God in the midst of you is a jealous God**—lest the anger of Yahweh your God be kindled against you, and He destroy you from the face of the earth (Deuteronomy 6:15).

In Hebrew, "qannā" is used both as a noun and adjective—meaning it is both a name of God and a description of His character and nature. In all of its different grammatical forms, the word for *jealousy* or *zeal* is used approximately 90 times in Scripture, 64 of which are positive (46 of these are humans who have godly jealousy).

The emphasis from the passages above describing God's character and name is that He is *actively* jealous. The name is used in the 10 Commandments (see Exodus 20:5 and Deuteronomy 5:9), and the word appears in Exodus 34:14 twice, but all six times the name *Qannā* is used, it is always in the context of having no other gods before Him.

THE REQUIREMENTS OF JEALOUSY

Unlike envy (which is an ardent desire to gain possession of something you don't currently have), jealousy is all about relationship. A literal understanding of jealousy is "an ardent desire to maintain exclusive devotion within a relationship in the face of a challenge to that exclusive devotion."[41]

In other words, jealousy is a passionate desire to guard and protect a relationship you already have. When a threat comes against the relationship, you rise up and protect the relationship.

So, to have jealousy, you need five things:
- love
- a lover
- a beloved
- a covenant relationship
- a threat to that covenant

God (the lover) has an indescribable love for His beloved (His people). He has made covenants with His beloved, yet there is a threat to that covenant relationship in the form of idols and the worship of other gods.

God is jealous over His people because they are His beloved and they bear His name (we are called CHRISTians). God wants His people to be faithful and is thus guarded against internal and external threats—anything that distracts their attention from Him.

I hope you see that jealousy in a relationship is NEEDED.

If a husband doesn't have godly jealousy for his wife and isn't willing to do whatever it takes to protect that covenant relationship, then when a threat appears (whether it be external, like a temptation to have an affair or look at pornography, or internal, like lust or bitterness), he is more susceptible to allow the threat into his marriage. But when a husband is jealous for his wife, he will do whatever is necessary to ensure that no threat can penetrate or compromise the covenant love and exclusive relationship he has with her.

Jealousy is needed not only in marriages but also in the church. I've never heard of a church requiring a potential pastor to have jealousy. Perhaps it seems a bit odd even to mention it, but when a pastor is jealous over his flock, he will stand against sin, compromise, distraction, and from wolves getting in and destroying the church (see Matthew 7:15 and Acts 20:28–31). To be blunt, if a pastor *doesn't* have godly jealousy in his life and ministry, he will allow the enemy entrance, let himself and his church be distracted from their devotion to Christ, and cause the name of the Lord to be blasphemed (see 2 Corinthians 11:2–3 and Romans 2:24). A church without godly jealousy is often the cause for a lack of church discipline or, to go the opposite, the harsh abuse of it.

We must remember the heart of godly jealousy is love with a passionate desire to protect the love relationship.

GOD'S INCREDIBLE JEALOUSY

As we examine the jealousy of God, here are a couple of points to consider:

God's jealousy is an act of His love.

God so loves the world that He gave His only begotten Son (see John 3:16), and anything threatening the relationship with His people causes Him to rise up and do something about that threat.

God is glorified by the faithfulness of His people; therefore, He responds with jealousy to anything that threatens that faithfulness and devotion.

In marriage, unfaithfulness between a husband and wife is called adultery. Unfaithfulness between God and His people is often termed adultery or idolatry.

Think back to how many times in Scripture, specifically in the Old Testament, the people of God turned from God to embrace idols. The book of Judges and nearly all the kings of Israel were marked by idolatry. Hosea was used as a demonstration of God's love and jealousy for His adulterous people, Israel, by marrying Gomer. The number one thing communicated in the prophetic books is "repent!" (same word as "turn" or "return")—found over 1000 times throughout the Old Testament (for example, see Jeremiah 18:11; Hosea 14:1; Joel 2:13; Ezekiel 18:30; 33:11)—and usually the prophetic call of repentance was due to idolatry and adultery with the world.

God is jealous for His people and refuses to allow anything to threaten that covenant relationship.

Do you see why God's jealousy is a benefit to us? If God weren't jealous, He would have left us long ago to our own devices and sin… but because of the great love with which He loves us, while we were still sinners living in rebellion, Christ died for us (see Romans 5:8). God is passionate and zealously guarded in His relationship with us!

God's name is Jealous, and that is a very good thing.

JEALOUS FOR GOD

What if we were jealous for God?

Elijah was jealous and stood for the honor of God before the prophets of Baal on Mount Carmel. David jealously removed the disgrace of Goliath from Israel. King Josiah jealously tore down the altars and idols Israel had set up.

What if we had a similar jealousy for God in our own lives?

If we were jealous for His name, character, reputation, and truth, it would cause us to be wholeheartedly devoted to Christ, profoundly pure, deeply humble, earnestly holy, and willing to boldly declare His truth and not care what others thought of us. In a culture that is marked by idols—called sports, money, success, sex, entertainment, etc.—jealousy for God would keep us from being distracted or interested in making those the gods of our lives. Sure, they in and of themselves and in their proper contexts aren't bad, but the moment they become your focus, your love, your rest, or your delight, they have become an idol, a god, and hence a threat to the covenant relationship you have with Jesus Christ.

Would you be willing to cast away the detestable things your eyes feast upon and not defile yourself with the idols of this world (see Ezekiel 20:7) but instead jealously guard your relationship with Jesus? Our God is Qannā. He is Jealous. And I, for one, am incredibly thankful He is.

GO DEEPER

1. Do you see how beautiful this concept is in light of what we discussed on day 20, that God is Jehovah Mekkodishkem (The Lord Who Sanctifies)? Because God is Qannā (Jealous), He refuses to allow anything to threaten His relationship with us, specifically sin—and yet He is also the One who brings about the sanctification and holiness in our lives. What an amazing God we have!

2. Read through the Scripture passages mentioned in today's study as well as Ezekiel 16, Matthew 21:12–13, John 2:14–17, and Acts 5:1–11. Make a list of further observations you find for God's jealousy and His desire to guard the covenant relationship He has with His people.

3. Are there idols, distractions, or sin in your life that must be jealously removed to guard your relationship with Jesus? Make a list of anything He brings to mind, repent of them, and rise up afresh to seek after the Lord jealously. Be aggressive in your willingness to remove anything that dishonors God. Phinehas, the grandson of Aaron, was jealous for the honor of God when he saw open rebellion before the Lord and aggressively

went in and slew the threat (see Numbers 25:6–8, 11; Psalm 106:28–31; 1 Corinthians 10:11). Though this was a physical example in the Old Testament, how can you be this zealous for the honor of God and, with aggressive jealously, remove any spiritual impurity and distraction from your life?

4. What is one practical thing you can do to keep a jealous guard and watch around your life from further threats?

DAY 27

WHAT DESCRIBES YOU?

The only explanation of my life should be Jesus.

That statement has captivated and convicted me over the past decade.

It comes from one of my all-time favorite quotes by a man obsessed with Jesus, Major Ian Thomas.

Ian Thomas, a major in the British military before becoming a preacher, had an infectious love and passion for Jesus. He had a simple way of sharing truth that would captivate an audience and leave them hungry for the life of Christ.

Thomas wrote in his book *The Mystery of Godliness*,

> *The Christian life can be explained only in terms of Jesus Christ, and if your life as a Christian can still be explained in terms of you—your personality, your willpower, your gift, your talent, your money, your courage, your scholarship, your dedication, your sacrifice, or your anything—than although you may have the Christian life, you are not yet living it!*[42]

DAY 27

The essence of Christianity is Christ!

God has called us to an impossible standard; we cannot live the Christian life in our own strength, wisdom, or ability. As Ian Thomas says, we need Christ to live the Christian life; in short, we need the indwelling life of Christ within us (i.e., the Holy Spirit).

You, in and of yourself, can mimic aspects of Christianity, but the only way you can fully live out the Christian life is by allowing Him to begin to live His life in and through you.

This is not about what you can do for Christ but what He wants to do in and through you to bring about His life, truth, and Gospel to the world. Yes, we are called to walk in obedience, to examine ourselves to see if we are in the faith, and to show ourselves approved—but not apart from Christ but IN Christ. This isn't passivity, but active dependence and abiding, as we live in Him and by His indwelling life.

Ian Thomas goes on to say…

> *If the way you live your life as a Christian can be explained in terms of you, what have you to offer to the man who lives next door? The way he lives his life can be explained in terms of him, and so far as he is concerned, you happen to be "religious"—but he is not! "Christianity" may be your hobby, but it is not his, and there is nothing about the way you practice it which strikes him as at all remarkable! There is nothing about you which leaves him guessing, and nothing commendable of which he does not feel himself equally capable without the inconvenience of becoming a Christian!…* **It has got to become**

obvious to others that the kind of life you are living is...beyond all human explanation! That it is beyond the consequences of man's capacity to imitate, and however little they may understand this, it is clearly the consequence only of God's capacity to reproduce Himself in you![43]

When someone looks at your life, can they explain how you live because of you (your talent, wisdom, ability, etc.)? What if the only explanation for how you live truly was Jesus? What if the peace you have amidst every circumstance, the joy you have in every trial, the boldness you have to stand for and proclaim truth, and the willingness to lay your life down and serve...could only be attributed to Christ in you?

As John the Baptist declared, "He must increase, but I must decrease" (John 3:30). Or as D.L. Moody quoted Henry Varley, "The world has yet to see what God can do with a man fully consecrated to Him. By God's help, I aim to be that man."[44]

What if the only explanation for your life was Jesus?

Today's Adventure:
Examine your life and consider whose resource, power, and ability it would be ascribed to. You or Jesus? Spend time with Jesus, repent for mimicking His life, and ask that He would freshly empower you through His indwelling Holy Spirit to live out Christianity as it was designed, in and through Him.

DAY 27

GO DEEPER

Consider studying these passages in light of the concept today:

- 2 Corinthians 4:5–11; 5:15–17; 11:3
- Galatians 2:20
- Philippians 2:13; 3:7–11
- Colossians 1:13, 26–27; 2:9–10; 3:3–4, 16
- 1 Peter 3:15

DAY 28

JEHOVAH SHAMMAH

Yahweh is There

At the end of his prophetic book, Ezekiel recounts the vision God gave him of the new Temple and city. Throughout chapters 40–48, Ezekiel sees, measures, and describes the immensity and beauty of the Temple and its city.

In chapter 47, he describes the ever-deepening river flowing from the Temple's threshold and running down into the Dead Sea, causing life to spring forth where there was only death before. The picture it creates is that of the Garden of Eden, a lush and fruitful land. Amazingly, death has been done away with, and now only life remains.

As Ezekiel concludes the vision and the book, he describes the city and ends with its name: *Jehovah Shammah*, Yahweh Is There.

EVERYWHERE YET SOMEWHERE

We know God is omnipresent and thus everywhere, yet Scripture also describes God as having a dwelling, a place where He is. Both are true—He is both everywhere and specifically somewhere.

Jeremiah reminds us, "'Am I a God who is near,' declares Yahweh, 'And not a God far off? Can a man hide himself in hiding places so I do not see him?' declares Yahweh. 'Do I not fill the heavens and the earth?' declares Yahweh" (Jeremiah 23:23–24).

Though God is everywhere and we cannot limit Him to a single locale, we find He specifically resided in the Tabernacle and then later in the Temple. And perhaps most astonishing, He was limited to a time and place in the form of humanity, Emmanuel, God with us, Jesus Christ, the Word made flesh.

God is everywhere, yet somewhere.

THE LORD IS THERE

Ezekiel tells us the name of a future city which God inhabits and dwells within—the city is known as the place where God is, Jehovah Shammah, for He, Yahweh, is there.

As Christians, shouldn't we also be known as the place where God dwells?

Jesus said to His disciples in the Upper Room, "...you know Him because He abides with you and will be in you.... On that day you will know that I am in My Father, and you in Me, and I in you" (John 14:17b, 20).

Jesus continued, "If anyone loves Me, he will keep My word; and My Father will love him, and We will come to him and make Our dwelling with him" (John 14:23).

I love the Greek word "dwelling" (monē)—sometimes translated as "home" or "abode"—it is the noun form of the verb "to abide" (menō). What is the home? It is the abode, the tabernacle, the dwelling, or the abiding place of God.

In John 15, Jesus talked about vine and branches and how the branch is commanded to abide in the life of the vine. The word "abide" (menō) gives the idea of "remain," "to hold tight to," "to rest in," or perhaps my favorite, "to refuse to depart." I also love how one Greek dictionary defines the word as an "inward, enduring personal communion."[45]

What are we commanded to do in Jesus? We are to refuse to depart from Him, rest and find our dwelling (life) in Him, and don't go anywhere—stay put (remain)! We must have an "inward, enduring personal communion" with Jesus Christ.

If Jesus resides within us through His indwelling Holy Spirit, and we have become His temple (see 1 Corinthians 3:16; 6:19), or, as Paul also calls us, "cracked pots," from which the glory and presence of God could shine through (see 2 Corinthians 4:7), shouldn't our lives reflect and demonstrate Him? I don't mean mimicking His life but *actually* having His life within us.

Do you know what we call people who live like that? We call them "Christians"—the people God indwells and inhabits.

We don't have to wait for a future city to see Jesus as Jehovah Shammah, though I'm excited for that day. Our lives and lips are to declare even now that He is alive, He dwells within us, and He is here.

DAY 28

GO DEEPER

1. Read John chapters 14–17 and consider it in light of God being Jehovah Shammah.

2. Are you making your dwelling (abode/home) in Christ? Are you "abiding" in Him? What can you practically do today to go deeper in your abiding relationship with Him?

3. If you want to take this idea further, I encourage you to read Andrew Murray's book *Absolute Surrender*, or at least the final chapter (*Ye Are The Branches*). You can find links for both at deeperChristian.com/30day.

Key Prayer Point: Ask Jesus to make you a pure vessel through which He can pour forth His life, light, love, and truth. Ask Him to reveal anything in your life that needs to be purified, removed, or transformed—and then repent of anything He reveals and walk in obedience to His Word. Don't allow any selfishness, pride, impurity, or sin to remain. Do you not know that you are a temple of the Holy Spirit, who is in you; thus, you are not your own, for you were bought with a price. So glorify God in your body—and in all you say, think, and do (see 1 Corinthians 6:19–20 and 10:31).

DAY 29

AS OINTMENT POURED FORTH

Today is our final day of looking at the names of God. With hundreds of names and titles throughout the Bible, we could spend the next couple of years meditating upon God's glory, majesty, and wonder *(which sounds like a lot of fun)*.

Throughout this adventure, I desired to introduce and lay a foundation for who our great God is. It is difficult to be amazed and breathless at the beauty of a sunset if you don't look at it; similarly, it's hard to be stirred by the majesty and beauty of Christ without beholding Him.

While we have given a simple overview of several names, there are countless more we haven't even mentioned, which I'd encourage you to find time to study at some point in your life (like you did back in day 23). Here is a short list to get you started:[46]

- El Shaddai (God Almighty)
- Jehovah Sabaoth (Lord of Hosts)
- El Hesed (God of Lovingkindness)
- El Roi (God Who Sees Me)
- Immanuel / Emmanuel (God with us)

DAY 29

Today, I want to take a panoramic view of the names of Jesus throughout Scripture. On day 4, I asked you to watch the video *He Is*,[47] which walks through many of Jesus' names chronologically. Today, I want to look at His names in thematic clusters.

AS OINTMENT POURED FORTH

The book *Song of Solomon* is a romantic poem about the love between a groom and his bride. The Jewish rabbis taught that the book was ultimately about God and His bride, Israel—and we know this has been fulfilled even more specifically with Christ and His bride, the Church (see Ephesians 5:31–32 and Revelation 19:7–8).

The main characters in Solomon's song of love are the groom (Solomon, the king) and his bride (often called the Shulamite—which should be translated as "Solyma," for the Hebrew is a feminine version of "Solomon"). This bride, a picture of the Church, who has taken on the name of the one she loves, says at the beginning of the book:

> *Because of the fragrance of your good ointments,*
> *Your name is ointment poured forth;*
> *Therefore the virgins love you.*
> **Song of Solomon 1:3 (NKJV)**

> *The fragrance of your perfume is intoxicating;*
> *your name is perfume poured out.*
> *No wonder young women adore you.*
> **Song of Solomon 1:3 (CSB)**

> *Your oils have a pleasing fragrance,*
> *Your name is like purified oil;*
> *Therefore the maidens love you.*
> **Song of Solomon 1:3 (NASB)**

> *Your anointing oils are fragrant;*
> *your name is oil poured out;*
> *therefore virgins love you.*
> **Song of Solomon 1:3 (ESV)**

The virgins (those who are set apart and live exclusively for their future beloved) love and adore the groom in the passage because His "name is like ointment poured forth."

As we've studied the names of God, have you grown in your awe and love of Jesus Christ? As perfume or precious oil poured forth, causing the fragrance to invade and consume its surroundings, the name of Jesus does the same thing…causing all those who are set apart for Him to love and adore Him more.

Below, you will see the names of Jesus organized (somewhat) by theme. Take time to slowly read through the names (even out loud) and behold, worship, and adore our Bridegroom and King.

Let this be a time of pouring forth His names like ointment.

Oh, my Precious Jesus, I worship You as Heavenly royalty. I love You as no mere man but as the King of all kings and the Lord of all lords. Your name is above every name and is like ointment poured forth.

DAY 29

You Are,
A Son given *(Isaiah 9:6),* **The Son of the living God** *(Matthew 16:16),* **The only begotten Son, which is in the bosom of the Father** *(John 1:18),* **The first-born of every creature** *(Colossians 1:15),* **The Son of the Highest** *(Luke 1:32),* **The Son of the Blessed** *(Mark 14:61)*

You Are,
The Mighty God *(Isaiah 9:6),* **The Everlasting God** *(Isaiah 40:28),* **The True God** *(1 John 5:20),* **God my Savior** *(Luke 1:47),* **Over all, God blessed forever** *(Romans 9:5),* **The God of the whole earth** *(Isaiah 54:5),* **God manifest in the flesh** *(1 Timothy 3:16),* **The great God and our Savior, Jesus Christ** *(Titus 2:13),* **Emanuel, God with us** *(Matthew 1:23),* **and Your throne, O God, is forever and ever** *(Hebrews 1:8)*

You Are,
The Almighty, which is, and which was, and which is to come *(Revelation 1:8),* **The Creator of all things** *(Colossians 1:16),* **The Upholder of all things** *(Hebrews 1:3),* **The Father of Eternity** *(Isaiah 9:6),* **The Beginning and the Ending** *(Revelation 1:8),* **The Alpha and the Omega** *(Revelation 1:8),* **The First and the Last** *(Revelation 1:17),* **The Life** *(1 John 1:2),* **That Eternal Life which was with the Father** *(1 John 1:2),* **He that lives** *(Revelation 1:18)*

You Are,
The Word *(John 1:1)*, The Word that was with God *(John 1:1)*, The Word that was God *(John 1:1)*, You are The Word of God *(Revelation 19:13)*, The Word of Life *(1 John 1:1)*, The Word that was made flesh *(John 1:14)*, The Image of God *(2 Corinthians 4:4)*, The Image of the Invisible God *(Colossians 1:15)*, The Express Image of His Person *(Hebrews 1:3)*, The Brightness of His Glory *(Hebrew 1:3)*

You Are,
A Child Born *(Isaiah 9:6)*, The Sent of the Father *(John 10:36)*, The Prophet of Nazareth *(Matthew 21:11)*, A Prophet mighty in deed and word *(Luke 24:19)*, A Servant *(Philippians 2:7)*, The Nazarene *(Matthew 2:23)*, The Carpenter *(Mark 6:3)*, A Stranger and an Alien *(Psalm 69:8)*, A Man of Sorrows *(Isaiah 53:3)*, A Worm, and no Man *(Psalm 22:6)*, even the Accursed of God *(Deuteronomy 21:23)*, who humbled Himself unto death, even death upon a cross *(Philippians 2:8)*

You Are,
Jesus *(Matthew 1:21)*, The Savior of the World *(1 John 4:14)*, A Savior, which is Christ the Lord *(Luke 2:11)*, Jesus Christ *(Revelation 1:5)*, The Lord Jesus Christ *(Colossians 1:2)*, Our Lord Jesus Christ Himself *(2 Thessalonians 2:16)*, Jesus the Christ *(Matthew 16:20)*, Jesus Christ our Lord *(Romans 5:21)*, Jesus Christ the Righteous

(1 John 2:1), **Jesus Christ, the same yesterday, today and forever** *(Hebrews 13:8),* **Jesus of Nazareth** *(Acts 22:8),* **Lord Jesus** *(Acts 7:59),* **Messiah** *(John 4:25),* **Anointed** *(Psalm 2:2; Acts 4:27),* **The Christ of God** *(Luke 9:20)*

You Are,
The Lamb of God *(John 1:29),* **A Lamb without blemish and without spot** *(1 Peter 1:19),* **The Lamb that was slain** *(Revelation 5:12),* **The Lamb in the midst of the throne** *(Revelation 7:17)*

You Are,
The Way *(John 14:6),* **The Door of the Sheep** *(John 10:7),* **The Shepherd of the Sheep** *(Hebrews 13:20),* **The Good Shepherd – that laid down His life** *(John 10:11),* **The Great Shepherd – that was brought again from the dead** *(Hebrews 13:20),* **The Chief Shepherd – that shall again appear** *(1 Peter 5:4)*

You Are,
The Vine *(John 15:5),* **The Tree of Life** *(Revelation 2:7),* **The Grain of Wheat** *(John 12:24),* **The Bread of God** *(John 6:33),* **The Bread of Life** *(John 6:35),* **The Hidden Manna** *(Revelation 2:17),* **A Plant of Renown** *(Ezekiel 34:29)*

You Are,
The Light *(John 12:35)*, The True Light *(John 1:9)*, A Great Light *(Isaiah 9:2)*, The Light of the world *(John 8:12)*, The Light of men *(John 1:4)*, A Light of the Gentiles *(Isaiah 42:6)*, A Star *(Numbers 24:17)*, The Bright and Morning Star *(Revelation 22:16)*, The Day Star *(2 Peter 1:19)*, The Day-spring from on High *(Luke 1:78)*, The Sun of Righteousness *(Malachi 4:2)*

You Are,
The Strength of the children of Israel *(Joel 3:16)*, A Strength to the Poor *(Isaiah 25:4)*, A Strength to the needy in distress *(Isaiah 25:4)*, A Refuge from the Storm *(Isaiah 25:4)*, A Covert from the Tempest *(Isaiah 32:2)*, The Hope of Your people *(Joel 3:16)*, A Horn of Salvation *(Luke 1:69)*

You Are,
The Rock *(Matthew 16:18)*, My Strong Rock *(Psalm 31:2)*, The Rock of Ages *(Isaiah 26:4)*, The Rock that is higher than I *(Psalm 61:2)*, My Rock and my Fortress *(Psalm 31:3)*, The Rock of my Strength *(Psalm 62:7)*, The Rock of my Refuge *(Psalm 94:22)*, A Rock of Habitation *(Psalm 71:3)*, The Rock of my Heart *(Psalm 73:26)*, The Rock of my Salvation *(2 Samuel 22:47)*, My Rock and my Redeemer *(Psalm 19:14)*, That Spiritual Rock *(1 Corinthians 10:4)*, A Shadow from the Heat *(Isaiah 25:4)*

DAY 29

You Are,
The Builder *(Hebrews 3:3; Matthew 16:18)*, The Foundation *(1 Corinthians 3:11)*, **A Sure Foundation** *(Isaiah 28:16)*, **A Stone** *(Isaiah 28:16)*, **A Living Stone** *(1 Peter 2:4)*, **A Tried Stone** *(Isaiah 28:16)*, **A Chief Cornerstone** *(1 Peter 2:6)*, **A Precious Stone** *(1 Peter 2:6)*

You Are,
The Minister of the Sanctuary and of the True Tabernacle *(Hebrews 8:2)*, The Minister of the Circumcision *(Romans 15:8)*, **and Your flesh is The Veil which was rent in two** *(Hebrews 10:20)*

You Are,
The Temple *(Revelation 21:22)*, **A Sanctuary** *(Isaiah 8:14)*, The Altar *(Hebrews 13:10)*, The Offerer *(Hebrews 7:27)*, The Offering *(Ephesians 5:2)*, The Sacrifice *(Ephesians 5:2)*, **and Your Life is A Ransom** *(Mark 10:49)*, **and You are The Lamb Slain** *(Revelation 13:8)*

You Are,
The Forerunner – where Jesus has gone on our behalf *(Hebrews 6:20)*, The Mercy Seat *(Romans 3:25)*, The Priest *(Hebrews 5:6)*, The High Priest *(Hebrews 3:1)*, The Great High Priest *(Hebrews 4:14)*, The Mediator *(1 Timothy 2:5)*, The Daysman *(Job 9:33)*, The Interpreter *(Job 33:23)*, The Intercessor *(Hebrews 7:25)*, The Advocate *(1 John 2:1)*, The Surety *(Hebrews 7:22)*

You Are,
The Gift of God *(John 4:10; 3:16)*, **His Unspeakable Gift** *(2 Corinthians 9:15)*, **The Chosen of God** *(Luke 23:35)*, **The Salvation of God** *(Luke 2:30)*, **The Redeemer** *(Isaiah 59:20)*, **The Shiloh, The Peace-Maker** *(Genesis 49:10)*, **The Most Blessed forever** *(Psalm 21:6)*, **And You are the One of whom the Father says, "My Beloved, in whom My soul is well pleased…** *(Matthew 12:18)*, **Mine Elect [Chosen], in whom My soul delights"** *(Isaiah 42:1)*

You Are,
Faithful and True *(Revelation 19:11)*, **The Truth** *(John 14:6)*, **A Covenant of the people** *(Isaiah 42:6)*, **The Covenanter** *(Hebrews 9:16, 17)*, **The Faithful and True Witness** *(Revelation 3:14)*, **A Witness to the People** *(Isaiah 55:4)*, **The Amen** *(Revelation 3:14)*

You Are,
The Holy One and the Just *(Acts 3:14)*, **The Holy One of Israel** *(Isaiah 49:7)*, **The Holy One of God** *(Mark 1:24)*, **Holy, Holy, Holy** *(Isaiah 6:3; John 12:41)*

You Are,
The Beginning of the Creation of God *(Revelation 3:14)*, **The First-Born from the dead** *(Colossians 1:18)*, **The First-Begotten of the**

dead *(Revelation 1:5)*, **The First-Born among many Brethren** *(Romans 8:29)*, **The First-Fruits of them that slept** *(1 Corinthians 15:20)*, **The Last Adam** *(1 Corinthians 15:45)*, **The Resurrection** *(John 11:25)*, **A Quickening Spirit** *(1 Corinthians 15:45)*, **The Head of the Body, the Church** *(Colossians 1:18)*, **The Head over all things to the Church** *(Ephesians 1:22)*, **The Head of every Man** *(1 Corinthians 11:3)*, **The Head of all Principality and Power** *(Colossians 2:10)*

You Are,
The Captain of the Host of the Lord *(Joshua 5:14)*, **The Captain of Salvation** *(Hebrews 2:10)*, **The Author and Finisher of Faith** *(Hebrews 12:2)*, **A Leader** *(Isaiah 55:4)*, **A Commander** *(Isaiah 55:4)*, **A Ruler** *(Micah 5:2)*, **A Governor** *(Matthew 2:6)*, **The Deliverer** *(Romans 11:26)*, **The Lion of the Tribe of Judah** *(Revelation 5:5)*, **An Ensign of the People** *(Isaiah 11:10)*, **The Chiefest among Ten Thousand** *(Song of Solomon 5:10)*, **A Polished Shaft** *(Isaiah 49:2)*, **The Shield** *(Psalm 84:9)*

You Are,
Lord of Lords *(Revelation 17:14)*, **Lord both of the dead and living** *(Romans 14:9)*, **Lord of the Sabbath** *(Luke 6:5)*, **Lord of Peace** *(2 Thessalonians 3:16)*, **Lord of all** *(Acts 10:36)*, **Lord over all** *(Romans 10:12)*

You Are,
The Messiah, the Prince *(Daniel 9:25)*, The Prince of Life *(Acts 3:15)*, A Prince and a Savior *(Acts 5:31)*, The Prince of Peace *(Isaiah 9:6)*, The Prince of Princes *(Daniel 8:25)*, The Prince of the Kings of the earth *(Revelation 1:5)*, The Glory of Your people Israel *(Luke 2:32)*, He that fills all in all *(Ephesians 1:23)*

You Are,
The King of Kings *(Revelation 19:16)*, The Judge *(Acts 17:31)*, The Righteous Judge *(2 Timothy 4:8)*, A Scepter out of Israel *(Numbers 24:17)*, David their King *(Jeremiah 30:9)*, King of the daughter of Zion *(John 12:15)*, born as The King of the Jews *(Matthew 2:2; 15:2)*, crucified as The King of the Jews *(John 19:19)*, The King of Saints, King of Nations *(Revelation 15:3)*, King over all the earth *(Zechariah 14:4, 5, 9)*, The King of Righteousness *(Hebrews 7:2)*, The King of Peace *(Hebrews 7:2)*, The King of Glory *(Psalm 24:10)*, The King in His beauty *(Isaiah 33:17)*, Crowned with a Crown of Thorns *(John 19:2)*, Crowned with Glory and Honor *(Hebrews 2:9)*, Crowned with a Crown of Pure Gold *(Psalm 21:3)*, Crowned with many Crowns *(Revelation 19:12)*, You sit enthroned as King forever *(Psalm 29:10)*

You Are,
A King and Priest after the Order of Melchizedek *(Hebrews 7:15-17)*, the One likened unto Moses

(Acts 3:22), **A Refiner's Fire** *(Malachi 3:2),* **Fuller's Soap** *(Malachi 3:2),* **You are the Light of the Morning when the sun rises, a morning without clouds** *(2 Samuel 23:4),* **You are as Rain upon the mown grass. As Showers that water the earth** *(Psalm 72:6),* **As Rivers of Water in a dry place. As the Shadow of a great Rock in a weary land. As a Hiding-place from the wind** *(Isaiah 32:2),* **You are as Ointment poured forth** *(Song of Solomon 1:3),* **Fairer than the Children of Men** *(Psalm 45:2)*

You Are,
The Bridegroom *(Matthew 9:15; Revelation 21:9),* **The Rose of Sharon** *(Song of Solomon 2:1),* **The Lily of the Valley** *(Song of Solomon 2:1),* **A Bundle of Myrrh** *(Song of Solomon 1:13),* **A Cluster of Henna Blooms** *(Song of Solomon 1:14)*

You Are,
A Crown of Glory and Beauty *(Isaiah 28:5),* **A Stone of Grace** *(Proverbs 17:8),* **A Nail fastened in a sure place** *(Isaiah 22:23),* **A Brother born for adversity** *(Proverbs 17:17),* **A Friend that sticks closer than a brother** *(Proverbs 18:24),* **A Friend that loves at all times** *(Proverbs 17:17),* **Your Countenance is as the sun** *(Revelation 1:16),* **Your Countenance is as Lebanon** *(Song of Solomon 5:15),* **Yes, You are altogether lovely. You are my Beloved and my Friend** *(Song of Solomon 5:16)*

AS OINTMENT POURED FORTH

When upon this earth you were,
Obedient *(Philemon 2:8)*, **Meek, Lowly** *(Matthew 11:29)*, **Guileless** *(1 Peter 2:22)*, **Tempted** *(Hebrews 4:15)*, **Oppressed** *(Isaiah 53:7)*, **Despised** *(Isaiah 53:3)*, **Rejected** *(Isaiah 53:3)*, **Betrayed** *(Matthew 27:3)*, **Condemned** *(Mark 14:64)*, **Reviled** *(1 Peter 2:23)*, **Scourged** *(John 19:1)*, **Mocked** *(Matthew 27:29)*, **Wounded** *(Isaiah 53:5)*, **Bruised** *(Isaiah 53:5)*, **Stricken** *(Isaiah 53:4)*, **Smitten** *(Isaiah 53:4)*, **Crucified** *(Matthew 27:35)*, **Forsaken** *(Psalm 22:1)*

But through it all, You are still,
Merciful *(Hebrews 2:17)*, **Faithful** *(Hebrews 2:17)*, **Holy, Harmless** *(Hebrews 7:26)*, **Undefiled** *(Hebrews 7:26)*, **Separate** *(Hebrews 7:26)*, **Perfect** *(Hebrews 5:9)*, **Glorious** *(Isaiah 49:5)*, **Mighty** *(Isaiah 63:1)*, **Justified** *(1 Timothy 3:16)*, **Exalted** *(Acts 2:33)*, **Risen** *(Luke 24:6)*, **Glorified** *(Acts 3:13)*

And You Are,
My Portion, My Maker, My Husband *(Isaiah 54:5)*, **My Well-Beloved** *(Song of Solomon 1:13)*, **My Savior** *(2 Peter 3:18)*, **My Hope** *(1 Timothy 1:1)*, **My Brother** *(Mark 3:35)*, **My Helper** *(Hebrews 13:6)*, **My Physician** *(Jeremiah 8:22)*, **My Healer** *(Luke 9:11)*, **My Refiner** *(Malachi 3:3)*, **My Purifier** *(Malachi 3:3)*, **My Lord, Master** *(John 13:13)*, **My Servant** *(Luke 12:37)*, **My Example** *(John 13:15)*, **My Teacher** *(John 3:2)*, **My Shepherd** *(Psalm 23:1)*, **My Keeper** *(John 17:12)*,

My Feeder *(Ezekiel 34:23)*, **My Leader** *(Isaiah 40:11)*, **My Restorer** *(Psalm 23:3)*, **My Resting Place** *(Jeremiah 50:6)*, **My Meat** *(John 6:55)*, **My Drink** *(John 6:55)*, **My Passover** *(1 Corinthians 5:7)*, **My Peace** *(Ephesians 2:14)*, **My Wisdom** *(1 Corinthians 1:30)*, **My Righteousness** *(1 Corinthians 1:30)*, **My Sanctification** *(1 Corinthians 1:30)*, **My Redemption** *(1 Corinthians 1:30)*, **My All in All** *(Colossians 3:11)*

You Are,
My Precious Jesus

DAY 30

WHAT'S NEXT?

Congratulations on finishing the 30 Day Adventure, but I need to tell you:
This is only the beginning.
My friend Eric Ludy calls it "The Endless Frontier."
As he tells it in his book *When God Writes Your Life Story*, Eric was taking vocal lessons from one of the best vocal coaches in the world, who never complimented him during the first year of training. So, one day, Eric got up the courage to ask how good he was. Scott, the vocal coach, replied:

"*Eric, you played soccer growing up didn't you?*"

"Yeah," I answered, *not quite catching what this had to do with my singing talents.*

"*When did you start playing soccer?*"

"I don't know. I guess I was probably seven."

"*Think back to when you were seven years old and you had been playing soccer for one month. How good were you?*"

"I stunk!" I answered without hesitation.

"Exactly!" Scott rang happily.

I stood there in stunned silence. Despair whirled

inside my head. After a year of intense training, I still stunk? All my hard work had been for nothing?

But before my self-deflating was complete, Scott interjected a powerful piece of wisdom. "Eric," he said earnestly, "there is something you need to understand. Singing is an endless frontier. It is a frontier that no one has reached the end of or fully explored. You have taken one step into this endless frontier, and you are asking me how far you have gone. Well, you've only taken one measly step!

"I want you to realize something," Scott continued sincerely. "You have taken one step into the endless frontier of singing. And you are now one step further into this frontier than 99.9 percent of the human race. But don't be satisfied with just one step. Don't settle for just being above average. Never pitch your tent. Until you have explored the outer reaches of this endless frontier, never stop your pursuit of excellence!"[48]

An endless frontier. That statement has forever changed Eric's life with singing and how he approaches every area of life: marriage, being a dad, and living as a Christian.

Most of us have taken one step into the endless frontier of Christ, looked back, and pitched our tent because we are one step ahead of the culture. But what if we saw the Narrow Way of the Cross for what it is: an adventure in an endless frontier?

Paul writes in Ephesians 3:17–19, "...so that Christ may dwell in your hearts through faith; and that you, being firmly rooted and grounded in love, may be able to comprehend with all the saints what is the breadth and length and height and depth, and to know the love of Christ which surpasses knowledge, **that you may be filled up to all the fullness of God.**"

He later says in 4:13, "…until we all attain to the unity of the faith, and of the full knowledge of the Son of God, **to a mature man, to the measure of the stature which belongs to the fullness of Christ…**"

This truly is an endless frontier. Oh, to know Him more!

When Andrew Murray was asked if he was satisfied in Christ, he responded,

"You will ask me, are you satisfied? Have you got all you want? God forbid. With the deepest feeling of my soul I can say that I am satisfied with Jesus now; but there is also the consciousness of how much fuller the revelation can be of the exceeding abundance of His grace. Let us never hesitate to say, 'This is only the beginning.'"[49]

Though we reached the end of the 30 Day Adventure, this is still only the beginning of knowing more of Christ. Don't pitch your tent.

Today's Adventure:
How do you plan to continue cultivating your relationship and intimacy with Jesus in the coming days? Be specific and commit to it.

I hope this simple study over the past thirty days has

been an encouragement and a blessing to your spiritual life. I pray it has pushed you another step down the endless frontier and given you a greater passion for continuing your pursuit of knowing Jesus—not just for academics but for intimacy, not for mere information but for transformation.

GO DEEPER

I have a deep love and passion for helping believers understand God's Word, grow in Christ, and live as genuine, bold, and victorious disciples of Jesus in today's world. If you would like additional resources and help to know Jesus more, I encourage you to check out my website, deeperChristian.com, where I release articles, podcasts, and other resources to help believers grow spiritually, know God's Word, have deeper intimacy with Jesus, and experience a Christ-centered life. I'd love to journey with you down the endless frontier.

ENDNOTES

1. Take this concept deeper by checking out my book, *Saturation Bible Study*.

2. C. H. Spurgeon, "God's Thoughts and Ours," (March 19, 1868) in *The Metropolitan Tabernacle Pulpit Sermons*, vol. 57 (London: Passmore & Alabaster, 1911), 188.

3. For suggested Bible reading plans, please see the bonus resources for this book at **deeperChristian.com/30day**

4. For resources to help you memorize the Bible, please visit **deeperChristian.com/30day**

5. David Martyn Lloyd-Jones, *God's Ultimate Purpose: An Exposition of Ephesians 1* (Edinburgh; Carlisle, PA: Banner of Truth Trust, 1978), 397.

6. "Moses and the Prophets" was a common Jewish phrase to refer to the entirety of the Old Testament, Moses being a symbol of the Law. This is confirmed at the end of Luke 24:27 when they say "all the Scriptures" (this was before the New Testament was written, so they spoke specifically of the entire Old Testament).

7. Roger Steer, *George Müller: Delighted in God* (Wheaton, IL: Harold Shaw, 1981), 160–61.

8. See **deeperChristian.com/30day** for resources, articles, and help to get started memorizing Scripture.

9   **biblememory.com** (use code DEEPER to get a discount off the Pro version, which also helps support the ministry of Deeper Christian and NRJohnson)

10 Learn more about my upcoming Bible study tours to Israel at **deeperChristian.com/israel**

11 "Peace" *New Oxford American Dictionary* (Oxford, United Kingdom: Oxford University Press, 2015).

12 Joshua M. Greever, "Peace," ed. John D. Barry et al., *The Lexham Bible Dictionary* (Bellingham, WA: Lexham Press, 2016).

13 Warren W. Wiersbe, *Be Available, "Be" Commentary Series* (Wheaton, IL: Victor Books, 1994), 51.

14 Elmer L. Towns, *The Ultimate Guide to the Names of God* (Grand Rapids, MI: Bethany House, 2014), 56–57.

15 Lyle Wesley Dorsett, *E. M. Bounds, Man of Prayer* (Grand Rapids, MI: Zondervan, 1991), 134. Also see: Edward Bounds, *The Necessity of Prayer* (annotated and updated edition) (Abbotsford, WI: Aneko Press, 2018), 48–52.

16 Leonard Ravenhill, *Why Revival Tarries* (Bloomington, MN: Bethany House, 1987), 27.

17 Ibid, 25.

18 John Wesley and Charles Wesley, *John and Charles Wesley: Selected Prayers, Hymns, Journal Notes, Sermons, Letters and Treatises*, ed. Richard J. Payne and Frank Whaling, The Classics of Western Spirituality (Mahwah, NJ: Paulist Press, 1981), 369.

19 Richard Foster, *Celebration of Discipline* (New York, NY: HarperCollins Publishers, 1998), 33.

20 E.M. Bounds, *Power Through Prayer* (Chicago, IL: Moody Press), 36.

21 Samuel Rutherford, *Letters of Samuel Rutherford* (Edinburgh; London: Oliphant, Anderson & Ferrier, 1891), 294.

22 Jim Cymbala, *Fresh Wind Fresh Fire* (Grand Rapids, MI: Zondervan, 2018), 84.

23 Mark Water, *The New Encyclopedia of Christian Quotations* (Alresford, Hampshire: John Hunt Publishers Ltd, 2000), 755.

24 D. A. Carson, *For the Love of God: A Daily Companion for Discovering the Riches of God's Word.*, vol. 2 (Wheaton, IL: Crossway Books, 1998), 49.

25 Wesley L. Duewel, *Touch the World Through Prayer* (Grand Rapids, MI: Zondervan, 1986), 195.

26 Oswald Chambers, *My Utmost for His Highest, September 16* (Grand Rapids, MI: Oswald Chambers Publications; Marshall Pickering, 1986).

27 Hesed is one of my favorite Hebrew words. It is often translated as mercy, love, steadfast love, loyalty, favor, faithfulness (and more than a dozen other words). My favorite definition comes from Michael Card's book *Inexpressible*, where he says that hesed is "when the person from whom I have a right to expect nothing gives me everything." Learn more about hesed at **deeperChristian.com/30day**.

28 Corrie ten Boom, *Tramp for the Lord* (Fort Washington, PA: Christian Literature Crusade, 1974), 55.

29 C. H. Spurgeon, "Divine Forgiveness Admired and Imitated," (May 17, 1885) in *The Metropolitan Tabernacle Pulpit Sermons*, vol. 31 (London: Passmore & Alabaster, 1885), 281.

30 Eric Ludy, *Power to Forgive* (sermon delivered at the Church at Ellerslie on July 1, 2012).

31 William Barclay, *The Letters to the Galatians and Ephesians, The New Daily Study Bible* (Louisville, KY; London: Westminster John Knox Press, 2002), 89.

32 John D. Barry et al., *Faithlife Study Bible* (Bellingham, WA: Lexham Press, 2012, 2016), Dt 6:5.

33 Jack S. Deere, "Deuteronomy," in *The Bible Knowledge Commentary: An Exposition of the Scriptures*, ed. J. F. Walvoord and R. B. Zuck, vol. 1 (Wheaton, IL: Victor Books, 1985), 274.

34 Gary M. Burge, *Jesus, the Middle Eastern Storyteller, Ancient Context, Ancient Faith* (Grand Rapids, MI: Zondervan, 2009), 23–25.

35 Aiden Wilson Tozer, *God's Pursuit of Man [The Divine Conquest]* (Camp Hill, PA: WingSpread, 2007), 5.

36 Elisabeth Elliot, *Through Gates of Splendor* (Wheaton, IL: Tyndale House Publishers, 1981), 20.

37 Oswald Chambers, *My Utmost for His Highest*, June 2 (Grand Rapids, MI: Oswald Chambers Publications; Marshall Pickering, 1986).

38 Ibid.

39 Helen Howarth Lemmel, *Turn Your Eyes Upon Jesus*, 1922.

40 The word appears twice in Exodus 34:14.

41 I got this definition from my friend Dan McConnaughey, who helped awaken me to this name's beautiful reality.

42 Ian Thomas, *The Saving Life of Christ and The Mystery of Godliness* (Grand Rapids, MI: Zondervan, 1988), 162-163.

43 Ibid.

44 Mark Fackler, "The World Has Yet to See …," *Christian History Magazine-Issue 25: Dwight L. Moody: 19th c. Evangelist* (Worcester, PA: Christian History Institute, 1990).

45 William Arndt et al., *A Greek-English Lexicon of the New Testament and Other Early Christian Literature [BDAG]*, μένω (Chicago: University of Chicago Press, 2000), 631.

46 I have an entire sermon series called *Behold Our God* which can be a great resource as you study more of God's names on your own. Find out more about the series at **deeperChristian.com/30day**.

47 You can find a link to the *He Is* video by going to **deeperChristian.com/30day**.

48 Eric and Leslie Ludy, *When God Writes Your Life Story* (Colorado Springs, CO: Multnomah Books, 2004), 25–26.

49 Andrew Murray, "The Exchanged Life" in *The Christian Magazine*, August 15, 1895.

www.ingramcontent.com/pod-product-compliance
Lightning Source LLC
Chambersburg PA
CBHW060748050426
42449CB00008B/1316